Pina Bausch and the Wuppertal Dance Theater

New Studies in Aesthetics

Robert Ginsberg
General Editor

Victor Yelverton Haines and Jo Ellen Jacobs
Associate Editors

Vol. 34

PETER LANG
New York • Washington, D.C./Baltimore • Bern
Frankfurt am Main • Berlin • Brussels • Vienna • Oxford

Ciane Fernandes

Pina Bausch and the Wuppertal Dance Theater

The Aesthetics of Repetition and Transformation

With a Foreword by RoseLee Goldberg
and a Preface by Susanne Schlicher

PETER LANG
New York • Washington, D.C./Baltimore • Bern
Frankfurt am Main • Berlin • Brussels • Vienna • Oxford

Library of Congress Cataloging-in-Publication Data

Fernandes, Ciane.
Pina Bausch and the Wuppertal Dance Theater: the aesthetics
of repetition and transformation / Ciane Fernandes.
p. cm. — (New studies in aesthetics; vol. 34)
Includes bibliographical references (p.) and index.
1. Tanztheater (Wuppertal, Germany). 2. Bausch, Pina.
3. Modern dance. I. Title. II. Series.
GV1786.T33 F47 792.8'2'092—dc21 00-066411
ISBN 0-8204-5251-3 (hardcover)
ISBN 0-8204-6705-7 (paperback)
ISSN 0893-6005

Die Deutsche Bibliothek-CIP-Einheitsaufnahme

Fernandes, Ciane:
Pina Bausch and the Wuppertal Dance Theater: the aesthetics
of repetition and transformation / Ciane Fernandes.
–New York; Washington, D.C./Baltimore; Bern;
Frankfurt am Main; Berlin; Brussels; Vienna; Oxford: Lang.
(New studies in aesthetics; Vol. 34)
ISBN 0-8204-5251-3

A Portuguese version of this work appeared in *Pina Bausch e o Wuppertal Dança-Teatro: Repetição e Transformação*, Hucitec, São Paulo 2000

Cover art: Wuppertal Dance Theater in *1980—A Piece by Pina Bausch*
© Photo by Gert Weigelt www.gert-weigelt.de

The paper in this book meets the guidelines for permanence and durability
of the Committee on Production Guidelines for Book Longevity
of the Council of Library Resources.

© 2001, 2002, 2005 Peter Lang Publishing, Inc., New York

To those who have danced this
and so many other creations with me.
Including you, reader.

What counts in the things said by [women and by] men is not so much what they may have thought or the extent to which these things represent their thoughts, as that which systematizes them from the outset, thus making them thereafter endlessly accessible to new discourses and open to the task of transforming them.

Michel Foucault, *The Birth of the Clinic*

It's hard for me to believe that I will die. Because I'm bubbling in a frigid freshness. My life is going to be very long because each instant *is*. The impression is that I'm still to be born and I can't quite manage it. I'm a heart beating in the world. You who read me, help me to be born.

Clarice Lispector, *The Stream of Life*

TABLE OF CONTENTS

ILLUSTRATIONS

FOREWORD

Texts invariably pass from hand to hand en route to publication. Friends or editors read finished sections before waving the material on to the next stage. Ciane Fernandes's *Pina Bausch* crossed continents on the way to the printer, accumulating commentary from individuals in Brazil, Germany, and the United States. The resulting book is a fascinating and multi-layered portrait of choreographer extraordinaire Pina Bausch, of her company the Wuppertal Dance Theater, and of the culture of late twentieth-century dance.

From introduction to appendices, Fernandes's inspired writing shows how nationalistic points of view, as well as academic tendencies of the 1980s and 1990s, have shaped our reading of Bausch's choreography. Susanne Schlicher, writing from Germany, is fascinated by Fernandes's South American interpretation of Bausch's work. She detects "a deep emotional understanding," and a "congeniality," that seems to have gone unnoticed in critical German writing on the artist, and she is surprised by the fact that Fernandes links a "structuralistic/poststructural discourse" to the movement theories of Rudolf von Laban, who had been largely forgotten in Post-Third Reich Germany.

Yet, Fernandes, who was born and performance-trained in Brazil and who studied at New York University and at the Laban/Bartenieff Institute of Movement Studies in the 1990s, makes connections between all of these, and more—between modern cultural theory and dance history, between a sixties European exploration of socio-political themes using an advanced ballet idiom, as devised by Kurt Jooss, with whom Bausch studied, and an American avant-garde that collapsed boundaries between disciplines, with collaborative experiments involving visual artists, composers and dancers, to whom Bausch was exposed when she studied at the Juilliard School of Music in New York in 1960.

Fernandes also has the necessary agility to follow wherever Bausch leads; in and out of psychoanalysis, movement, language, and silence. Fernandes articulates a range of methods that Bausch has developed for the gestation and execution of her full-scale productions. And she has stayed close to Bausch's dancers, questioning them with a dancer's need to know, from the inside, exactly how a movement is made. She has even followed particular productions over time: Fernandes saw *Kontakthof*

(1978) twice within a ten-year period, and we benefit from her thoughtful investigation into how the work was changed by a "constant process of repetition," and by the personal histories of different dancers.

Fernandes builds a complex map of Bausch's body language, her working methods, and the emotional undertow of Bausch's dance philosophy, without losing the reader. That she also provides mini-portraits of such paragons of the Wuppertaler Tanztheater, as Jan Minarik, Anne Marie Benati, or Mechthild Grossmann, makes this a highly readable text. For those of us lucky enough to have seen Bausch's work, Fernandes's descriptions of the players, and what they were thinking as they danced, and of the space of the stage, conjure up visual and visceral memories from a storage bank of images and movement. For those who have yet to experience Bausch live, Ciane Fernandes's writing provides a rich and fascinating introduction.

RoseLee Goldberg
Critic, curator, and author of *Performance Art from Futurism to the Present*;
Teacher at New York University

PREFACE

Pina Bausch and her Wuppertaler Tanztheater, as well as the former German *Ausdruckstanz* (German expressionistic dance) in general, find a special deep understanding in South America. This congeniality is characterized in Ciane Fernandes's present book in which she investigates the many emotional, aesthetic, and performance-related implications and functions of repetition in the works of Pina Bausch. Fernandes analyzes the emotional attraction with an analytical discourse, using the theories of Jacques Lacan and Michel Foucault, in order to discuss Bausch's work simultaneously on an aesthetic, philosophical, psychological, and social levels.

In German dance-writing, a post-structuralistic theoretical framework is not common, especially as it relates to *Tanztheater* and choreographers such as Bausch. Post-structuralist theories have been only recently brought into the discourse on dance, mainly reflecting contemporary dance and the works of a young generation of choreographers such as Sasha Waltz, Xavier Le Roy, Thomas Lehmen, and Jerome Bel. Interestingly, this new theoretical frame has also been brought forward by a young generation of dance writers for whom *Tanztheater* would seem to be history.

Also new to the German dance audience is Fernandes's linking of structuralistic/post-structuralist discourse to the movement theories of Rudolf von Laban—one of the founders of German modern dance and dance theater, and a multitalented personality. Laban's writings, theories about space harmony and movement dynamics, and his Labanotation, provided dance—especially modern dance of the twentieth century—a strong base that remains relevant. With this, he contributed strongly to the emancipation and recognition of dance as an independent art form. Fernandes revisits the works of Laban, demonstrating how his theories, especially the Laban Movement Analysis (LMA), have created the foundations for future generations to explore both the symbolic *and* the linguistic nature of dance.

Due to the political and artistic break forced by the Third Reich, World War II, and the emigration of many artists (among others Rudolf von Laban and Kurt Jooss), the Laban movement theories were not well-known in post-war West Germany. His analytical system is only vaguely addressed in the writing about German *Tanztheater*—mostly indirectly via the work of Jooss, one of his famous students and collaborators. In general, the Laban heritage is not present in the country in which he had developed his main theories during the first three decades of the twentieth century. It exists more as a hidden knowledge somehow preserved in the pedagogical work of some dance teachers and a few select schools. This includes the Folkwang School in Essen and the Lola Rogge School in Hamburg, two former Laban schools that have survived since the 1920s.

Ciane Fernandes's use of LMA knowledge in her analytical discourse about Pina Bausch's work has not been available in Germany in either scientific or journalistic reception of *Tanztheater*. LMA was developed in the United States in the early 1970s, carrying on Laban's work in England of the 1940s and 1950s. It is only recently that a LMA program has started in Germany, which is based in Berlin and is mostly attended by freelance dancers, physiotherapists, and movement/dance therapists. Here the applications are restricted mostly to dance pedagogy and therapy. LMA is still to reach the curriculum of German universities.

The above situation often comes as a surprise to the dance community outside Germany, not familiar with post-war developments in that country. German society did not want to refer back to its famous national heritage of modern dance history of the 1920s and 1930s. Instead, it longed for international classical ballet. It was only through the success of *Tanztheater*, of choreographers such as Pina Bausch, Reinhild Hoffmann, and Susanne Linke, that we rediscovered our own modern dance history. Then we started research on German *Ausdruckstanz*, on the work of Mary Wigman, Kurt Jooss, Rudolf von Laban, and many others. So far, our research is still in its infancy.

On the other hand, at the turn of the twenty-first century, German *Tanztheater* seems to have become a historical phenomenon in itself. It covers more than three decades of productions by the first generation of choreographers—Pina Bausch, Gerhard Bohner, Reinhild Hoffmann, Hans Kresnik, Susanne Linke—as well as of following second and third generations. Aesthetically, as well as socio-historically, *Tanztheater* is posited in the 1970s and 1980s, originating during the initial confrontation with the political and cultural situation of post-war West Germany in the 1960s. American Performance Arts, Happening, or (post)modern dance from the United States, rightly and carefully pointed out by Fernandes, only appear as marginal influences in the German reception of *Tanztheater*.

In Germany, *Tanztheater* is known to be rooted in the context of the 1968 upheavals, and the following drastic aesthetic changes in post-war German drama theater. These changes had been postulated by a young generation that took over the position of theater director, and as an extension, the power in city theaters all over Germany. Two of the leading figures were Peter Zadek and Peter Stein, supported by stage designers Erich Wonder, Wilfried Minks, and Karl Ernst Herrmann. They all opposed the declamatory theater of the 1950s, represented by icons such as Gustaf Gründgens and Will Quadflieg, presenting instead theater that was highly visual, physical and often anarchic/chaotic.

Dance theater and drama theater did influence each other. Dance took advantage of the new aesthetics of images, the open structure, and the emancipation from a narrative story line. It also used the cinematic principles and the awareness of reality and everyday-life presented in contemporary drama theater. On the other hand, drama theater considered dance theater as a non-repressive, non-hierarchical language, allowing for a physical-emotional way of (self-)expression and experience onstage. Besides the aesthetic influences, drama theater again mystified dance and movement language as natural, authentic, pre-expressive, and pre-verbal. This tendency was supported by the fact that contemporary theater was posited in the discourse of the *Frankfurter Schule*, in the theories of Horkheimer/Adorno and Herbert Marcuse.

Contemporary theater as well as *Tanztheater* were also placed within the theories of civilization as stated by Norbert Elias and Rudolf zur Lippe, where civilization is described as a process of increasing repression of the spontaneity of the body, emotions, and psyche, and of the expression of human nature. Although discussed in this framework, the choreographers of *Tanztheater* never claimed to be presenting or searching for an authenticity of the body or for a so-called natural movement language. In her book, Fernandes proves this statement. In addition, her book shows that dance theater, with its understanding of movement and dance as both natural energy and linguistic communication, opposes the idealization and mystification of the body, its specific logic, and articulation.

Fernandes offers a third avenue for exploring dance theater. She does not ignore the multiple reality and the proper logic of the body, but brings them into the discourse as a new layer. Fernandes demystifies dance and movement by examining on all levels of performance the deconstructive effects of Bausch's Tanztheater, articulated in her pieces especially through repetition. Fernandes's model is the Lemniscate, a three-dimensional spatial figure that was introduced to dance by Laban. The Lemniscate is fundamental to the construction of nature and life, including the process of moving and thinking, of re-presenting and re-constructing body memories and social history.

The Lemniscate shape allows Fernandes to fragment Laban's philosophy and relocate part of it. Fernandes isolates the LMA system and replace it within the poststructuralist discourse of Lacan and Foucault. In Fernandes's book, LMA and Lacan's signifying chain challenge and re-define each other, suggesting that the language of dance for which they are searching is an as intrinsically dynamic and changeable system, as is the Lemniscate shape. This also follows for the process of writing about dance in the context of theory.

The real experience of the book is that: As a reader, you are taken along a path that is not linearly straight, but that has a meandering way of going in and out of Bausch's works. In one page, you are placed in the middle of a piece; in the next you are exposed to a very analytical point of view; and in the following page, you are presented with the dancers' personal explorations in an interpersonal context.

Due to her experience as both performer and academic, Fernandes is able to devote herself equally to both worlds: the emotionality of Bausch's nonverbal world of images, and the theoretical verbal world provided here by Lacan, Foucault, and Susanne K. Langer. Through a highly analytical discourse, Fernandes succeeds in keeping sensibility, respect, honesty, and humility toward the world of movement and images. The author becomes herself a mediator between dance and theory, movement and words, aesthetics and analysis. The descriptions/explorations of scenes taken from different pieces of Bausch provide the reader, who maybe not has seen one of her pieces, with many possibilities to experience the artistic variety of the Wuppertaler Tanztheater.

Susanne Schlicher

Dramaturg, author of *TanzTheater: Traditionen und Freiheiten*;
Coordinator of Department of Theater Directing, University of Hamburg

ACKNOWLEDGMENTS

This has been a creative process of rewriting and transforming movement and/into words, with the help of a multimedia staff. For the extensive revisions, I acknowledge the great help of Narendran Chanmugam and Matthias Lütkehermölle; as well as Jacqueline Pavlovic, David Iannitelli, Mara Peets, and Robert Sember. I am very thankful to Rainer Brueckheimer, Sônia Roncador, and Simone Erbeck for the translations.

I am especially thankful to Ruth Amarante, Julie Shanahan, Regina Advento, Dieter Feldkamp, and Maria Teresa Amarante, for their input, candor, and friendship. I thank Alberto Roveri, Euler Paixão, Francesco Carbone, and Gert Weigelt for the permission to reprint their high quality artwork. I am thankful to Peter Anders, Jochen Viehoff, Maarten Vanden Abeele, Urs Kaufmann, and Matthias Schmiegelt.

For the encouragement and academic support in the earlier version of this work (New York University, 1995), I am in debt to my professors Miriam Berger, Mark Franko, Marianne Goldberg, RoseLee Goldberg, Jackie Hand, Jonathan Kalb, Gabriel Moran, Robert Sirota, Robert Taylor, and Susanne K. Walther. Eliene Benício, Armindo Bião, Sérgio Farias, Suzana Martins, Leda Muhana, and Eliana Rodrigues have made this work possible by their professional support at the Federal University of Bahia, Brazil.

The following special friends participated in the process of this work: Jurema Alvarez, Olívia Araújo, Kátia Canton, Eliana Carneiro, Douglas Dunn, Diane Elshout, Ricardo Fagundes, Carlos Fernandes, Rosel Grassmann, Frank Händeler, Wagner Lacerda, João Lima, Aline Lira, Regina Miranda, Rogério Moura, Lusergio Nobre, Cristiane and Osni Omena, Susanne Schlicher, Lívia Serafim, Nana Shineflug, and Flávio Venturini.

During the research years, some of the institutions that became a second home include: Brooklyn Academy of Music, Dance and Dance Education Program of New York University, Dance Collection at the Lincoln Center Public Library for the Performing Arts, Goethe Institute (New York and Salvador-Bahia), and Laban/Bartenieff Institute of Movement Studies. I am especially thankful to the Brazilian Agency for the Improvement of Higher Education Personnel (CAPES) and its professionals, for its financial support during the research.

1

GERMAN DANCE THEATER:
AESTHETIC CONSIDERATIONS

I think each person has to discover dance on his or her own. One cannot give advice. Each one has his or her way of choreographing. Of course it is very beautiful to have a rich variety of possibilities, something linking the different arts. But I cannot tell if this is or not the best way; it can be many things together in harmony. To form schools is dangerous, because it stops the fantasy. It seems important to me that people change the moments of their lives. The feeling about what is happening in the world is always a new moment.

    Pina Bausch (in an interview with Cristina Durán, 1994)

Only later did I realize, as in this instance—the fact of referring to myself with conviction as a choreographer—is very important. Consider Kandinsky and his abstract forms. If he had called himself a graphic artist, no one would have minded. Calling himself a painter, he provoked and prevented the world of painting from a sleepy tranquility. The choice cleared up my doubts. I simply told myself that dance could have new rules.

    Jean-Claude Gallotta (quoted in Kerkhoven, 1991)

This book is an aesthetic and theoretical exploration of repetition in the works of the contemporary German choreographer Philippine "Pina" Bausch (b. 1940, Solingen; figure 1). She became director of what was then called Ballett der Wuppertaler Bühnen in 1973, and through her innovations had its name changed to Wuppertaler Tanztheater. She has then become the leader of *Tanztheater* (dance theater), an artistic trend of remarkable importance in contemporary performing arts (Schlicher, 1987; 1993), and recently she has been considered the most important choreographer of the twentieth century (Schmidt 1998).

    The origins of German dance theater can be traced back to the works of Rudolf von Laban (1879–1958) and his pupils Mary Wigman and Kurt Jooss (Partsch-Bergsohn 1994). In the 1920s and 1930s, Laban used the term "dance theater" to describe dance as an independent art form, based on harmonious correspondences between the dynamics of movement and spatial pathways (1971 and 1988). Nevertheless, his

Figure 1. Pina Bausch
© Photo by Euler Paixão

movement system developed out of "Dance-Tone-Word Improvisations" (*Tanz-Ton-Wort*), in which students borrowed from other art forms, using voice, creating small poems, or dancing in silence (Osborne 1989, 90). The resulting dance pieces incorporated both everyday and pure movement in a narrative, comical, or more abstract form.

Wigman founded *Ausdruckstanz*, German expressionistic dance. This was a rebellion against classical ballet and a search for an individual expression linked with universal human struggles and needs (Howe, 1987; 1996). For further references on Mary Wigman consult Wigman (1966) and Manning (1993).

Jooss developed sociopolitical themes through dramatic group action and precise formal structure and production (Markard and Markard 1985). The training of dancers under his direction combined music, speech education, and dance, using elements of classical ballet and Laban's theories of space harmony and movement dynamics (Walther, 1990; 1993; 1994).

Also relevant to the history of German dance theater was Bertolt Brecht's theater theories and practices concerned with sociopolitical themes. Brecht's "epic theater" included concepts such as "Gestus," V-effect, montage techniques, and unexpected comic moments. Brecht's concept of Gestus or "Gebärde" emphasized a complex and many times contradictory combination of both body actions and words as a "socially significant gest, not illustrative or expressive" (1979, 198). Through such effects, Brecht's epic theater provoked the spectators' recognition of daily situations and facilitated their actions and decision-making toward change. Other theater directors who opened up avenues for contemporary dance theater by emphasizing the body were Samuel Beckett (Connor 1988) and Antonin Artaud (1958).

Bausch's work combines her training with Jooss at the Folkwang School and as a soloist in his Folkwangballett with her experience in the arts and dance in New York in the 1960s. Bausch studied ballet until age fifteen, when she went to the Dance Department of the Folkwang School in Essen, directed by Jooss. In 1960, she went to the Juilliard School of Music, New York, as a special student. Bausch's teachers in 1960–1961 included Antony Tudor, José Limón, Anna Sokolow, Alfredo Corvino, Margret Craske, Louis Horst, and La Meri. Simultaneously, she became a member of the Dance Company Paul Sanasardo and Donya Feuer. In 1961, Bausch was engaged by the New American Ballet and the

Metropolitan Opera, and also collaborated with Paul Taylor. In 1962, she returned to Germany and became a soloist and choreographer of the Folkwangballett, directed by Jooss. In 1969, Bausch took over the direction of the former Folkwangballett, since then called Folkwang Tanzstudio. In 1973, she became the director of the Ballett der Wuppertaler Bühnen, which had its name changed to Wuppertal Tanztheater. During the 1980s, she became the director of the Dance Department of the Folkwang School.

During her years in New York, many American dancers and choreographers reacted against techniques of modern dance and joined visual artists and musicians to produce collaborative works. These expressed sociopolitical concerns about civil rights, the environment, and feminism, and also questioned the nature of art. Artists intended to tear down the separation between art and everyday life, and between performers and audience. The collaborative pieces involved daily body movements and costumes, in a critique of formal and artificial theatrical representation (Haskell 1984). In these interactive works of the 1960s, "Collage techniques were used instead of plots...patterns of sounds or movement were used in repetition to create hypnotic effects...choreographers focused now on the pedestrian movements observing basic human relations of ordinary people" (Partsch-Bergsohn 1988). Jooss and American works of the 1960s emphasize human relations, daily movement vocabulary, and collaboration between different art forms.

Bausch has been influenced by the collaboration between the arts in both her European and American experiences. As mentioned in Thomas McEvilley's review of *1980—A Piece by Pina Bausch*, she "revives the Dada performance vocabulary and brings it to life with astonishing vigor" (1984, 85). During the first decades of the twentieth century, the interaction between the different art fields was a main quality of the European avant-garde movements, such as Dada and Bauhaus (Goldberg 2001). These movements developed close to and sometimes interacted with dance theater (Prevots 1985). Laban was an architect and designer, and his notation symbols resemble those of Russian constructivist painting.

Bausch's works transcend these influences. Her pieces include the interaction between art forms in a critical manner. As in the works of the 1960s, her pieces present an overall group chaos under certain order, favoring process over product. Unexpected experiences are also evoked by the pieces, involving both dancers and audience. Yet Bausch's works achieve such qualities without rejecting the theatrically grandiose.

Bausch's association of technical form with emotional content, and entertainment with critical art, approaches Jooss's philosophy:

> We are living in an age which is rediscovering artistic form. In dance this means that out of the chaos of arbitrary and haphazard movements [of *Ausdruckstanz*] only the essentially important ones will be developed....A creative compromise between free personal expression and formal compliance with objective, intellectual laws is developing: a compromise in the noblest sense, which can also be described as axial to the world of art. (Jooss in Markard and Markard 1985, 16–17)

Bausch's interaction between the arts happens in a majestic, augmented manner, closer to that of large-scale opera or ballet-theater productions or even cinema (for further reference, see Kawin 1989). The relationship between Bausch's dance theater and cinema can also be seen in her film *The Plaint of the Empress* (*Die Klage der Kaiserin*, 1989). Onstage, the strong visual and auditory impact of her pieces often projects cinematic impressions onto the audience. Such majestic images surprisingly give place to nearly empty, dim, and silent stage-scenes.

The dancers' elegant evening costumes and makeup add to the majestic setting. Instead of wearing simple daily clothes of inter-arts works of the 1960s, or unisex leotards of abstract dance, Bausch's dancers are dressed up as if attending a social event. Their costumes and makeup set up their social and gender roles, invoking the audience's expectations for a grand spectacle. However, in many of scenes, dancers just walk, chat, perform slight movements, or interact with the audience, unfulfilling these expectations and instigating desire for "dance" movement.

In the 1960s, the body-politics was that of a provocative nudity interacting with other arts in other environments outside of the stage (Warr and Jones 2000). Differing from that, Bausch's dance theater stimulates nostalgia for a *Belle Époque*, making fun of these concepts of beauty imposed on the body. Stereotypes of characters from progressive periods such as the 1930s, Hollywood personalities in fur coats and tuxedos, or full skirts of the American 1950s, are critically exposed. Her works are presented in strange and compulsive gestures and contexts. For instance, physical collision and hysterical screams fill out an entire scene, a dancer makes an enormous "live sandwich" by placing one of her legs between pieces of a long loaf of bread, a group dances the twist, exaggerating it to absurdity.

The use of organic material, such as water, mud, carnations, or salt on the floor resembles the inter-arts of the 1960s, albeit in a larger production scale. These objects are not used to integrate the body with nature, but are obstacles—dancers move gingerly around these elements or even among urban objects such as bricks from a ruined wall (*Palermo, Palermo,* 1989), or chairs and tables (*Café Müller,* 1978). Differing from Wagner's *Gesamtkunstwerk* (integrated work of art), in which various artistic elements were intended to complement each other, in Bausch's works such elements are brought onstage as independent entities, stretching the borders of dance (Jeschke and Vettermann 2000). For instance, curtains open and close, dancing to the loud sound of a strong symphony in the background; thirty-two pine trees are brought onto the stage, and independently begin to fall to the ground in successive impacts, in a dance of de-forestation.

Differing from the works of the 1960s, Bausch's pieces do not intend to break the barriers between performance and life. She incorporates live elements and daily movements precisely to demonstrate that they are as artificial and representational as are stage performances. As will be shown later, she accomplishes this through the repetition of both movements and words. Spontaneity is an unexpected and unforeseeable experience that can only happen through such repetition.

Bausch's choreography incorporates and alters ballet's form and content by using the dancers' life experiences together with technical or everyday movements. Her work approaches that of Wigman in its use of the dancers' personal experiences, and surpasses Wigman by critically using ballet technique and not denying it. Similar to the dancers under Jooss, Bausch's performers are well trained in ballet, but are older—in their thirties or forties—with more experience in life and dance.

Laban defined dance as "human movement [that] creates compositions of lines in space which, from a definite start, show a structural development, a build up leading to a climax, a solution and an ending" (Bartenieff 1980, 191). This implies a sense of completion or integration. Bausch departs from this approach, structuring scenes through collage technique in free association. Small movement sequences or scenes are fragmented, repeated, alternated, or performed simultaneously without a clear build-up toward a closing solution.

Repetition is a crucial method and subject of Bausch's Tanztheater. Through repetition of movements and words, Bausch confirms and alters the tradition of German dance theater—exploring the nature of dance and theater, and of their psychological implications:

> The history of theatre can be traced back to the beginning of European civilization (of Greek theatre). It has always been part of, and protected by, a culture based on language; a culture which for a long time was convinced that everything, or almost everything, could be said with words. The history of dance is much harder to piece together due to the fact that dance cannot be recorded in writing....[Today] there is still a tendency to consider actors as the intellectuals of the stage, and dancers as spontaneous beings able to enter into contact with the hidden forces of the universe. Our minds still cling to the idea that inside each man there is a rift between mind and body. Body/mind, heart/head—in these binary constructions we find once more the basic masculine/feminine dichotomy. (Kerkhoven 1993, 30)

Since its beginning, German dance theater has broken this convention of both theater and dance. In Laban's dance theater, the dancer was an integrated "thinking-feeling-acting being" (Bartenieff 1970, 11). Laban's method was founded primarily on "'thinking in movement' which developed a consciousness and an awareness that is not to be confounded with a cognitive or intellectual approach, for it demanded that the dance experience be understood, felt and perceived by the individual as a complete being" (Osborne 1989, 94). Such integration is part of the training in Laban Movement Analysis (LMA) up to today. It is defined as the student's ability to express himself or herself verbally and physically through LMA, with personal and emotional involvement (Laban/Bartenieff Institute of Movement Studies, 1994). Along with this philosophy of dance, Laban created a system of notation for the understanding of dance as a kinetic symbolic language, different from spontaneous expression or discursive language (Laban 1975). For Laban, dance has a "meaningful, understandable content" (Bartenieff 1980, 191). His framework can be paralleled to Susanne K. Langer's theory. According to Langer, every work of art consists of a "symbolic language"—the means through which feelings are articulated (1953, 31).

In Bausch's works, dance and theater are also presented as a symbolic language, though not as a body-mind or form-meaning totality and completion as defined by Laban. Instead, the linguistic natures of dance and theater are explored as intrinsically fragmented. Through fragmentation and repetition, Bausch's works expose and explore the gap between dance and theater in aesthetic, psychological, and social levels. Gestures and words do not complement each other providing clear communication; the body does not complete the mind to create a whole self; female and male do not form a unity liberating the individual from loneliness. Repetition breaks the popular image of dancers as "spontaneous beings," revealing their dissatisfactions and desires within a chain of repetitive movements and words.

Gestures are body movements onstage or in everyday life, and are part of an everyday language associated with mundane activities and functions. Onstage, gestures gain an aesthetic function; they become stylized and even technically shaped, within specific vocabularies such as ballet or American modern dance. In her works, Bausch uses everyday and technical gestures. However, in many instances, through repetition daily gestures become abstract movements.

When a gesture is done for the first time onstage, it can be (mis)taken as spontaneous expression. But when the same gesture is repeated several times, it is clearly exposed as an aesthetic element. In the first repetitions, it becomes apparent that gesture is dissociated from a spontaneous emotional source. Eventually, the exhaustive movement repetitions generate feelings and experiences for both dancer and audience. During the course of repetitions, meanings are transitory, emerging, dissolving, and being altered. Repetition enables a constant change of dance theater within Lacan's Symbolic order (1988, 220–233).

Differing from Langer's symbolic language, Lacan's Symbolic order refers to the linguistic developmental stage of the narcissistic ego. While in Langer's symbolic language form corresponds to meaning, Lacan's Symbolic order includes self-referential signs, multipliers of meanings within a "signifying chain" (Lacan 1978, 42–52). As in Lacan's Symbolic order, words in Bausch's pieces are repeated until their literal meaning is dissolved. Eventually, the body and its anatomy, as well as pathologies and pains, are evoked by those same words. Through repetition, theatrical means—words—become references to the physicality of dance.

Similar to Laban's dance theater, Bausch's work intertwines dance and words that is not an intellectual approach. Differing from Laban's concept of integration or oneness, Bausch's work implies a constant incompleteness, search, and transformation within the thinking-feeling-acting fragmentation and multiplicity:

> The steps have always come from somewhere else—never from the legs....It is simply a question of when is it dance, when is it not. Where does it start? When do we call it dance? It does in fact have something to do with consciousness, with bodily consciousness, and the way we form things. But then it needn't have this kind of aesthetic form. It can have a quite different form and still be dance. Basically one wants to say something that cannot be said [for the expression of the inner material would imply its transformation into language], so what one has done is to make a poem where one can feel what is meant. And so words, I find, are a means—a means to an end. (Bausch in Servos and Weigelt 1984, 235, 230; also in Servos 1996, 294)

Defined as "bodily consciousness" and "the way we form things," dance theater's symbolic nature is associated with physical and psychological human development. As Lacan asserts, it is through language that the ego not only interacts with the world, but also is itself constructed in its body image (1977, 1–7).

According to Lacan, body image is formed by successive internalization of specific outside images, beginning in early childhood. The construction of this "body map" does not depend upon biological laws, but on parental signification and fantasies about the body. The body image is a repetition of the environmental or social familial mapping in the person's psyche and physical organs. It is the means by which the schema of gestures and postures of society is transmitted. Personal body identity is not authentic or contrasting to society. The personal body is a social body—a social construction at psychological and physical levels, constantly permeated and controlled by repetitive discipline within social power relationships.

Through repetition, Bausch exposes dance theater's symbolic nature, and explores the body map acquired through repetition from childhood to adolescence. The dancers of the Wuppertaler Tanztheater often re-enact moments from their childhood during performance, showing the audience how they incorporated social patterns. Onstage, they repeat the instances in which they started repeating other people's movements and behaviors. They enact "childlike fears in childish games and ritual, sometimes all playing at children, sometimes playing adults and children" (Wright 1989, 116).

Through repetition, Bausch's dance theater carries forward both Wigman's concerns with personal and psychological expression and Jooss's social and political concerns. It also expands Brecht's social *gestus* into personal body politics:

[Although] Pina Bausch's dance theatre...uses some of the basic concepts of epic theatre—*gestus*, V-effect, a certain employment of the comic as a sudden switch of gestalt...her political goals are different....The difference is that her actors show themselves; the split they enact between body and social role is experienced and enacted on their own bodies. They are the demonstrators of their own bodies [with their histories], not the body of some passer-by, as in Brecht's street-scene model. (Wright 1989, 118–119)

For further references to Bausch's transcendence of Brecht's works, see her reconstruction of his *The Seven Deadly Sins* (*Die sieben Todsünden*, 1976) and Roth (1986).

To re-enact past scenes in present performance is to reconstruct the subject's body history, transforming it into an aesthetic form:

The fact that the subject relives, comes to remember, in the intuitive sense of the word, the formative events of his existence, is not in itself so very important. What matters is what he reconstructs of it....The subject's centre of gravity is this present synthesis of the past [realized in performance] which we call history. (Lacan 1988, 13, 36)

Through repetition of gestures, words, and past experiences, Bausch's dance theater can be defined as the body's consciousness of its history as a symbolic and social subject in constant transformation. She has stretched the borders not just of dance but also of all the arts, creating a space that fluctuates between theater, dance, music, film, performance art, happening. Her works are constructed through and by the body in its proper "logic"—fragmented, multiple, incoherent, and complex. In doing so, she has influenced an extended set of contemporary artistic explorations, such as those of Anna Theresa de Keersmaeker, Wim Vandekeybus, Meg Stuart, Alain Platel, among others (Goldberg 1998; Schmidt 2000). Federico Fellini describes his reaction to Bausch and one of her pieces:

...with her aristocratic, tender and cruel, mysterious and familiar aura, closed in an enigmatic immobility, Pina Bausch smiled at me to make herself known. What a beautiful face! One of those faces destined to be fixed, gigantic and perturbing on the film screens....I watched her performance from beginning to end and wished it had been longer. I immediately felt a great empathy, an accomplice with an unequalled grace, of a cheerful breeze that blew across the scene. (Hoghe and Weiss 1980, back cover page)

From Symbol to Sign:
The Language of Dance

But I'm trying to write you with my whole body, shooting an arrow that firmly pierces the tender nerve ends of the word. My incognito body tells you: "Dinosaurus, icthiosaurus and plesiosaurus," word with a merely auditory sense, without turning into dry straw but staying moist. I don't paint ideas, I paint the more intangible "forever." Or "for never," it's the same. Above all else, I paint painting.
   Clarice Lispector (1989)

To find a language. For dancing. For life. "Only talking does not mean anything," Pina Bausch said in a rehearsal, and at another event, "Caressing can also be dance." In her work she is searching and always finding another language / not only for dancing. The approach to this new language is very subtle and with a great respect for dance. "That [in dancing] what I find beautiful and important and valuable I want to leave untouched in the first moment because I find it so important."..."I think one needs to learn dance again—or one has to learn something else first and maybe then one can dance again.
   Raimund Hoghe and Pina Bausch (quoted in Erler, 1994)

Dance: Between the Natural and the Verbal

According to Karl Otto Apel, philosophical history can be divided into three stages: ontological, epistemological, and linguistic (Samuels 1993, 3). The ontological, begun by Plato (427–347 B.C.), was interested in objects themselves. The epistemological, begun by René Descartes (1596–1650), was concerned with the subject of knowledge or ego. And in the linguistic, begun by Ludwig Wittgenstein (1889–1951), philosophers have been concerned with the issue of language and social relations (Edwards 1990). In the twentieth century, within this linguistic stage, the understanding of human movement, and consequently dance, has oscillated between natural expression and linguistic code system.

According to Susanne K. Langer, dance's connection to the human body and its independence from verbal language has led to many (mis)interpretations of dance as the only art form capable of a direct expression: "The widely popular doctrine that every work of art takes rise from an emotion that agitates the artist, and which is directly 'expressed' in the work, may be found in the literature of every art....Only in the literature of the dance, the claim to direct self expression is very nearly unanimous" (1953, 176). Susan L. Foster describes this aesthetic attitude in the history of contemporary dance:

> The quest for a natural way of moving, a natural body and a natural, organic choreographic process dominated American concert dance in the early part of this [twentieth] century, and it continues today. Typically, those engaged in this quest accord dance a role as the most appropriate medium of expression for primal, emotional, and libidinal dimensions of human experience. Dance is seen as an outlet for intuitive or unconscious feelings inaccessible to verbal (intellectual) expression. Based on this model, dancers often cultivate a sanctimonious mutism, denying what is verbal, logical, and discursive in order to champion the physical and the sensate. (1986, xiv–xv)

In opposition to this interpretation of spontaneous expression, human movement is seen as a system of learned social communication parallel to verbal language. The first suggestion of body movement corresponding to the words of a language was made by Charles Darwin in 1872. This thesis was developed in the late 1940s and early 1950s by American Kinesics, a structuralist science of the study of body behavior (Birdwhistell, 1952; 1970). Today's Kinesics is based mostly on Edward Sapir's thesis that "corporal gesture is a code that must be learnt with a view to a successful communication" (Kristeva 1978). Studies in this area have tried to measure body movement ("nonverbal language") by comparing it to "verbal language," attributing meanings to selected gestures (Sebeok and Umiker-Sebeok 1981).

In the "naturalist" view, as referred by Foster, body movement precedes and is uninfluenced by verbal language. Yet, the "linguistic" interpretation favors verbal language. Both interpretations deny the paradox of dance and movement of being simultaneously physical and linguistic.

> The human body is a locus of the relation between passion and action, between impression and expression, between perception and movement. It is a

projection screen for imaginary obsessions and the proximate instrument of fantasies pressing for incarnation and realization. The body oscillates; it is not solely a field, not solely a medium. It can be described and it can speak. It fluctuates between symptom and symbol. The oscillation probably describes the figure eight of a Möbius strip. It is never visible in its entirety. (Kamper 1988, 46)

The strict naturalistic or verbal interpretation do not allow a critical exploration of the power relationship and constant reciprocal influence between words and movement in both dance and everyday life. A theory that questions such a power relationship requires a redefinition of language beyond the purely verbal. Such a theory would include dance's foremost contradiction—its tangible physicality as an abstract system of signs—without positing itself as an absolute. Such paradoxical understanding of movement and dance as natural energy and as linguistic communication is part of Bausch's philosophy, and best suits the analysis of her works:

It is very important, it is fantastic, for people to use the joy of movement [in everyday life]. It is necessary to use all the energies in life. Sometimes we receive too much pressure, and where does it go? Or we do something positive, or not so much, with all this energy, or we simply do not know what to do with it. But it is also something that should happen in group, because people meet, communicate. (Bausch in Cristina Durán, 1994).

Laban and Langer: Dance Theater as Symbolic Language

The discussion of body movement as either natural or linguistic has always been a special part of German dance theater. Since its beginning, choreographers were concerned with the definition and exploration of a language of dance. Such language would be different from spontaneous, unmediated expression, and from verbal language. Laban's main concern was to define dance theater within such "principles":

When I undertook as the first one among dancers of today to speak of a world for which language lacks words, I was fully aware of the difficulty of this undertaking. Only a firm conviction that one has to conquer for dance the field of written and spoken expression, to open it up...to widest circles, brought me to tackle this difficult task. (1920; in Maletic 1987, 51)

Laban's theories of movement can be seen as an attempt to integrate dance's "mystical" quality with the scientific approach of structuralism and linguistics at the beginning of the twentieth century. Laban intended to establish principles, derived from a "symbology [particular to]...dance forms," in order to "capture, preserve, examine [dance's] ephemeral creations" (Maletic 1987, 113). His structuralist attitude aimed to establish dance as an autonomous art form with its own language. Paradoxically, his attempt to emancipate dance also resists dance's inherently ephemeral quality, while trying to solve the anxiety of a constant movement loss.

Laban's theory of movement—the basis for his system of notation—is parallel to Langer's concept of symbolic language (Bartenieff 1970). According to Langer, all art forms consist of "an imagined feeling, or a precisely conceived emotion that is formulated in a perceptible symbol," different from "a feeling or emotion actually experienced in response to real events" (Langer 1953, 181). The movements carried out by the dancer are real, in terms of neural-muscular activity, being logically expressive instead of self-expressive. "The dancer's actual gestures are used to create a semblance of self-expression, and are thereby transformed into virtual spontaneous movement, or virtual gesture" (1953, 180). Virtual gesture, based on imagined or conceptualized feeling (not necessarily experienced) constitutes the primary illusion of dance, defining it as an art form.

The definition of dance as "symbolic language" and "virtual gesture" liberates it from the naturalistic and linguistic views. Nonetheless, it establishes the correspondence between meaning ("import") and form, in a Saussurean structuralist organization. According to Ferdinand de Saussure (1916), language (*langue*) is a system of signs that are divided into concept or "signified," and its corresponding (auditory, visual or graphic) external representation, or "signifier." These two units relate as in the formula:

$$\frac{\text{signified}}{\text{signifier}}$$

This correspondence insures language as a unit contained in itself, that successfully structures and organizes personal expression and social relations.

Consistent with the above formula, Laban considered each "movement tension" as an expression of a corresponding feeling or emotion, and each written symbol as an expression of a corresponding gesture:

> [E]very emotional state coincides with a very definite body tension....In every gesture and its symbolic representation [notation] the basic form elements stay the same: the straight line, the wave, the spiral. Their differentiation and the combinations result in different context of feeling and thought. (1920; in Bartenieff 1970, 10)

Laban also defended the correspondence between body and mind in a "complete being" through this symbolic gestured language (Osborne 1989, 94).

Laban's symbols and terminology for movement description were intended to be as dynamic as dance, rather than static units:

> *Choreographie* [first formulation of choreutics and movement notation, 1926]. The explanation of the world of dance forms must not be confined to an enumeration of rigid states. This world must be considered as undulations (waviness, transformation) alive with constant change. (1920; in Bartenieff 1970, 5)

To pursue such "dynamic" notation, Laban based his movement theories on a "continuum between polarities," such as mobility-stability, and inner-outer (Maletic 1987, 52). Just as in the symbolic correspondence between feeling and form, and between movement and notation, or body and mind, such polarities related within a unifying whole.

Bausch and Lacan: Dance Theater as Signifying Chain

Bausch's works agree with Laban's theory in positing dance as language, but they alter Laban's unifying theories of form-meaning and body-mind. While the theories of Laban and Langer imply the unification and meaningful fulfillment of the "symbol," Bausch's dance theater explores the arbitrariness and the unrest of the "sign":

> In the case of the symbol the signified object is *represented* by the signifying unit through a restrictive function-relation; while the sign...pretends not to

assume this relation which in its case is weaker and therefore might be regarded as arbitrary. (Kristeva 1986, 64)

For Julia Kristeva, the symbol is "anti-paradoxical," since its two opposing units (represented and representation) form a closed circuit of direct correspondence and totality. The sign, instead of expressing a corresponding feeling, is able to refer to many meanings, or return to itself. In the case of the sign, the totality and fulfillment of the symbol is substituted by fragmentation, ambiguity, absence of corresponding sense, and self-repetition. The sign only concedes meaning in a form that is relational, arbitrary, and unpredictable. It becomes a form about its own structure; it speaks about itself, multiplying instead of closing itself in a single meaning. Liberated from its corresponding sense, the sign creates a (language) system marked by repetition and transformation:

> The sign can create an open system of transformation and generation...[it] signifies an infinitization of the discourse...it becomes a potential mutation, a constant transformation...not as something caused by extrinsic factors [such as preexisting feelings or meanings], but as a transformation produced by the possible combinations [*combinatoire*] within its own structure...its meaning is the result of an interaction with other signs...within its field, new structures are forever generated and transformed. (Kristeva 1986, 71, 72)

Through the repetition of movements or words, Bausch's works expose the gap rather than correspondence between expression and perception. They insist on dance's constant change and lack of preservation.

In Langer's theory of art, signification is only possible through a correspondence between form and content (symbolic language). As in Langer's theories, the content of Bausch's works can only be born from their form. Nonetheless, in Bausch's pieces, repetition constantly detaches meaning from their initial form. Meanings are discarded and challenged rather than conveyed by the repetitive form. In this sense, repetition in Bausch's works places dance within Lacan's signifying chain, surpassing Langer's symbolic language.

Lacan inverted the Saussurean's formula, putting the signifier in capital letter and roman type, and the signified in italic type underneath it (1977, 149):

S (SIGNIFIER)
s (signified)

Within the domain of the signifier, language does not communicate a clear meaning. Instead of conveying an *a priori* signified, the signifier multiplies and generates unpredictable meanings, which can only come from a relationship between signifiers (metonymy and metaphor). Kristeva's system of "infinitization of discourse" agrees with Lacan's concept of the "signifying chain":

> Anyone who goes in search of meaning at its source, or in its essential forms, has no choice but to travel by way of language, and at every moment on this journey variously connected signifiers extend to the horizon in all directions. When the signified seems finally to be within reach, it dissolves at the explorer's touch into yet more signifiers. (Bowie 1991, 64)

For Lacan, language is simultaneously verbal and corporal; it is not limited to verbalization, or to gestures correspondent to words. Language is a system of socio-familial constructions that builds the individual's psychological and physical body. Structured in a chain, language is an invasive and distorting mediator, and a multiplying and transformative source. Lacan places dance—either everyday or technical movements—within this paradoxical signifying chain: "Now, a human gesture does belong with language and not with motor manifestations" (St. Augustine in Lacan, 1988, 255).

A Language in Movement

Although Laban's theories are based on unified polarities, Laban Movement Analysis (LMA) can be updated and placed within the context of body-mind and movement-feeling independence common to the works of both Bausch and Lacan. In such a manner, movement description does not form a unity with its movement source. There is necessarily a gap between the LMA description and the dance. Research done in this area does not attempt to describe the dances with absolute precision, or to preserve them. Instead, the research opens new possibilities of understanding of the dances within the Symbolic search (Lacan). Instead of establishing corresponding symbols and meanings,

LMA multiples the possibilities of interpretation and theoretical associations, and enhances the creation of writing and dancing material. LMA becomes a "pluralizing semantic power": a linguistic, artistic, and philosophical tool (Bowie 1991, 66).

Laban's search for a "dynamic" language seems more accomplished within Lacan's constantly transformative signifying chain than within the Saussurean's unified and correspondent oppositions. Within the signifying chain, Laban's binary oppositions attempt to reflect each other, searching for an Imaginary mirroring completion (Lacan). But they reciprocate disturbance and change in each other. Within the signifying chain, the relationship between Laban's binary oppositions becomes a transformative "process on a continuum" of re-definitions and searches.

Such dynamics within the Symbolic order can be best represented by the geometric figure of the Moebius Strip already cited by Dieter Kamper (1988, 46) in the beginning of this chapter, and utilized by both Rudolf von Laban and Jacques Lacan. This shape is described by Laban as "Lemniscate" (1974, 98) and by Lacan as a three-dimensional shape without a center (1977, 105). It corresponds to a three-dimensional eight figure created from the junction of the two inverted extremities of a strip, in which the faces become simultaneously internal and external. It was discovered by A. F. Moebius (1790–1868), who described it as "having no 'other side,' i.e., a surface on the one side of which one can get to its other without crossing an edge" (Moebius in Laban 1974, 98; figure 2).

Laban described the Moebius Strip in terms of dance, where two parts of the body perform different and harmonious movements:

> An intermediary stage between the knot and the simple twisted line is the lemniscate. Knot-lines and twisted-lines can form the edge of lemniscatic bands. Such bands have not clearly distinguishable inside or outside surfaces. They are twisted band-circles. When we observe people move it, it frequently seems as if they have the desire to nestle in a curved plane or an arched band, or to stroke it. Planes, bands and also lemniscates can be recognized by their double-line trace-forms concurrently made by two parts of the moving limb or the trunk. This is like a "duet" of two parts of the body as in two-part singing....We have to move along the whole band twice in order to return to the point of departure, twisting at the same time. (1974, 97–98)

Figure 2. The Moebius Strip or Lemniscate Shape
© Photo by the author

Even today, the Lemniscate is used in LMA within new developments of Laban's theories (Hackney 1998, 34, 35, 156, 214).

Lacan uses the shape to represent the fall of the individual in the Symbolic order and signifying chain, where the individual and the "other" (Ragland-Sullivan 1986, 16) constantly fail to meet:

> To say that this mortal meaning [the fall into the Symbolic] reveals in speech a centre exterior to language is more than a metaphor; it manifests a structure. This structure is different from the spatialization of the circumference or of the sphere in which some people like to schematize the limits of the living being and his milieu: it corresponds rather to the relational group that symbolic logic designates topologically as an annulus.
> If I wished to give an intuitive representation of it, it seems that, rather than have recourse to the surface aspect of a zone, I should call on the three-dimensional form of a torus, in so far as its peripheral exteriority and its central exteriority constitute only one single region. (Lacan 1977, 105)

This philosophical encounter between poststructuralist psycho-analysis (Lacan) and structuralist movement-analysis (Laban) results from the application of Bausch's method of fragmentation and repetition. The present book fragments Laban's philosophy, separating his notation "system" from his structuralist framework. The poststructuralist framework poses LMA with a disturbing rather than completing "double"—a similar but challenging self-reflection (Laban/Lacan). Within the Lemniscate shape, Laban Movement Analysis and Lacan's signifying chain challenge and re-define each other in a constant search for the language of dance. Such a "relocation" of Laban's theory within a poststructuralist framework does not stray from his original project:

> In conclusion one may suggest that due to the breadth of his original conceptions, Laban's movement classification provides a sufficiently broad basis for both further development of his germinal ideas and for its application within other theoretical frameworks. (Maletic 1987, 184)

Bausch's method fragments and repeats elements of different art forms from either everyday life or theater. Within this setting, the elements distort each other rather than provide an apparent and Imaginary completion (Lacan). In the distorting mirror structure of her pieces, the repetition of movements and words constantly changes each other, multiplying their significance. Within the inverted eight figure of the Symbolic, Bausch's works deal with several continuous dynamics rather than stable dichotomies: *repetitiontransformation, dancetheater, signifiersignified, movementwords, bodymind, womanman, individualsociety, futurepast, selfother*—all written without cuts or separations, as in the Moebius Strip.

The "infinitization of the discourse" (Kristeva) and the signifying chain (Lacan) suggest language to be an intrinsically dynamic and changeable system. Applied to dance, this model liberates body movement from conveying feelings or meanings. It enables dance to use its own medium—body movement—to explore itself as an art form. The dancing body questions its natural or linguistic constitution. The categorization of body movement as preceding or being dominated by verbal language is substituted by a critical exploration of the categorization *per se*. Dance is neither a spontaneous expression of instincts nor the object of scientific speculation. In the signifying chain, dance is the exploration, the criticism, and the search for its own mediums.

Following the models of Lacan and Kristeva, dance is a constant search between physicality and language, making it inherently double and paradoxical. As in Lacan's theory, the Real (the physicality of dance), the Imaginary (the image projected by dance), and the Symbolic (language and dance's other—theater, words) coexist, constantly challenging and re-defining themselves:

> The Symbolic, the Imaginary and the Real pressurize each other continuously and have their short-term truces, but they do not allow any embracing programme for synthesis to emerge inside or outside the analytic encountered. The three orders together comprise a complex topological space in which the characteristic disorderly motions of the human mind can be plotted. Plenitude is to be approached not by the ever more ambitious movements of dialectical synthesis in the Hegelian manner, but additionally—by reading off one by one the interference between Symbolic, Imaginary and Real by which "human being" is defined. (Bowie 1991, 98–99)

Thus, the language of dance is the criticism of any scheme of fixed and final principles. It is the language of the paradox, the language of a non-language.

Writingdancing

The Moebius Strip is an apt conceptual-spatial representation for the study of Bausch's works. With this research model, theory and practice are not opposing, but challenge and recreate each other in a process of *writingdancing*—Sally Banes's title (1994) included in the Moebius Strip—and "working through" of gestural and verbal language. In accordance with the principle of *repetitiontransformation*, the expression "working through" refers to a continuous process of exploration of the resistance and repression, in opposition to "compulsive repetition" and "recollection" which do not transform the repetitive pattern (Freud, 1963). Jacques Lacan added "working through language" (1988, 21–23) to Freud's terminology.

Repetition has been addressed as a crucial part of human existence in the writings of major thinkers, including Plato (Tate 1928), Kierkegaard (1843), Freud (1958), Heidegger (1962), Benjamin (1976), Derrida (1978), Deleuze (1994), among others (Caputo 1987). I have chosen Lacan and Foucault due to the relevancy of their theories in the post-modern context, especially when applied to Bausch's compositions. Lacan has gone beyond Freud's concepts of "repetition compulsion" and "working through," intertwining society and the psyche through the linguistic construction of a "body schema." In the same way, Foucault posits the concept of "docile bodies," constructed by repetitive social discipline and medical discourse. Similar to Bausch's works, these two philosophers have outlined the body as constructed by language and beyond spontaneous expression.

The present book makes use of the methods of analyzing dance of structuralism and post-structuralism. It follows distinct categories, but it also allows for a flexible interrelation between the categorized elements, and for the emergence of various—and at times contradictory—meanings.

The scenes selected for analysis are taken mostly from four pieces: *Kontakthof* (1978), *Arien* (1979), *1980—A Piece by Pina Bausch* (*1980—Ein Stück von Pina Bausch*, 1980), *On the Mountain a Cry Was Heard* (*Auf dem Gebirge hat man ein Geschrei gehört*, 1984). In addition, the following works are also discussed: *Iphigenie auf Tauris* (1974); *Orpheus und Eurydike* (1975); *The Rite of Spring* (*Frühlingsopfer*, 1975); *The Seven Deadly Sins* (*Die sieben Todsünden*,

1976); *Bluebeard—While Listening to a Tape Recorder of Béla Bartók's Opera "Duke Bluebeard's Castle"* (*Blaubart—Beim Anhören einer Tonbandaufnahme von Béla Bartóks Oper "Herzog Blaubarts Burg,"* 1977); *Café Müller* (1978); *Bandoneon* (1980); *Waltz* (*Waltzer*, 1982); *Carnations* (*Nelken*, 1982); *Two Cigarettes in the Dark* (1985); *Palermo, Palermo* (1989); *The Plaint of the Empress* (*Die Klage der Kaiserin*, 1989); *Dance Evening II* (*Tanzabend II*, 1991); *A Game of Sadness* (*Ein Trauerspiel*, 1993). For a recent chronology of Bausch's works, see Vogel (2000).

The scenes were initially organized into two overall categories of repetition: Formal Repetitions, and Reconstructive Repetitions. Formal Repetitions include: The exact repetition of a movement phrase ("obsessive"); the repetition of a scene with subtle changes ("altered"); the repetition of the same event in different contexts ("intermittent"); the repetition of previously separated events simultaneously in the same scene ("long-range"). Reconstructive Repetitions include the reconstruction of the dancers' past experiences (mainly from childhood) and the reconstruction of a traditional tale or opera. Such reconstructions do not necessarily include the formal repetition of movement and words in performance.

In each chapter, these categories are organized according to their degree of complexity, beginning with solos and duets leading up to group scenes. Bausch's works include both categories with their alternating and even simultaneous effects. This book applies Bausch's choreographic method (see chapter 2), selecting some movement sequences and repeating them in different contexts according to its aesthetic and literary objective.

The movement analysis done in this book follows Hutchinson-Guest (1983), and Moore and Yamamoto (1988). Following the LMA system, the dancer is the point of reference when indicating areas on the stage, that is, the dancer's left, right, front, etc., and not those of the audience.

2
THE CREATIVE PROCESS:
(DIS)ASSEMBLING CHARACTERS AND SCENES

"Something about your first love."
"How did you, as children, imagine love?"
"Two sentences about love."
"How do you imagine love?"
"When someone forces you to love, how do you react, then?"
"Key word: Love your brother as your own self."
"Once more a little contribution to the Love Theme."
  Bausch's questions from rehearsals for *Carnations* (1986/1987)

In the way I work and do the pieces, difference always appears. It is this: my way of working always makes things happen differently. It is as if it were every time a different piece and at the same time the same one, unique. It is hard to say how or where anything changed, because it is all very organic. The changes happen without the need to wake up with an idea. Everything can change suddenly. When I do a new creation, it springs, it does not matter how. The important thing for me is life, everything I meet. I like to go to new places, have experiences, see theater pieces, but this is not necessarily a help, because they are things already made, they already happened and I have to do my own things.
  Pina Bausch (in an interview with Cristina Durán, 1994)

In systematized dance techniques such as classical ballet and many modern dance forms, repetition is part of dance training and the creative process. Daily repetition of pre-set exercises and movement sequences is a basic method for technical training. During the creative process of dance pieces, some choreographers use repetition as a formal compositional tool, in order to connect movements and movement phrases. Many choreographers use repetition to teach sequences to the dancers. In order to memorize the sequences, dancers repeat the movements with the choreographer and then by themselves. In this way, repetition constructs a movement vocabulary on the dancers' body, which will then become a vehicle for the technical dance form. More often, dance professionals (teachers, choreographers, and dancers) rearrange and confirm (repeat) already existing movement vocabularies.

In Bausch's creative process, repetition is not used to confirm or deny the vocabularies imposed on the dancing bodies. Instead, repetition is used to dismantle such movement vocabularies learned either by dance techniques or socialization. Repetition becomes a creative tool through which dancers reconstruct, unsettle, and transform their aesthetic and social background. Repetition initially fragments the dancers' experiences and the narrative of their movement sequences. Eventually, repetition creates a different kind of continuity, transforming the histories of the dancers' bodies as well as the audience's (pre)conceptions and perceptions of its own body history.

Repetition is a structural part of the Wuppertal Dance Theater's creative process. Initially, repetition comes about as the aesthetic reconstruction of the dancers' past experiences. This reconstruction is not based on the expression of a present feeling, but in the description— symbolic translation—of past feelings. Extensive repetition of the personal scenes gradually shapes them into an aesthetic form, dissociated from the dancers' personality. In stage performance, the repetitive scenes created through such rehearsal process may evoke diverse themes and experiences for performers and viewers.

Beginning with *Bluebeard* (*Blaubart,* 1978), Bausch's pieces have all been created with the dancers' participation. To induce their creative contribution, Bausch may present them with a question, a theme, a word, sound, or phrase: "Talking to a flower," "Mourning," "Ah!" (Amarante, appendix A). In response to these elements, the dancers improvise in any means they desire: movement, words, sound, or a combination of elements, with some questions to be answered only in the form of movement.

At the beginning of the first rehearsal for *Bandoneon* (1980), Bausch gave the dancers an open task:

> Just a simple sentence. It can be a question if you like. Anyway, not a long sentence. Write it down somewhere. You shouldn't change it later. Just playing, acting with gestures. Try to express what you have done. You can also make it simpler; even change the order....Just see if you can get across to us with gestures. So, let's see if we understand. (Wildenhahn 1982)

One by one, the dancers stepped forward to express their sentences in gestures until they were understood by the others. In this way, the choreography is initiated by the dancers' exploration of their experiences (meaning) and means of expression (form). Although starting with words—"a simple sentence"—the exercise's real task is to translate them into personal and social body language (Hoghe and Weiss 1989, 10).

Many of Bausch's questions relate to past experiences: "how was our childhood...an important person in our lives or childhood....Many questions are about how it was in our countries, culturally specific questions" (Amarante, appendix A). These questions place the dancers' personal remembrances in their social and cultural settings. Other questions address the dancers' emotional life more directly, also implying remembrance. Such questions awaken the dancers' emotional memories, transforming them into symbolic language.

To begin the seventh day of rehearsal for *Bandoneon*, Bausch asked:

Tell me, describe to me: When you cry, how do you cry? What you do when you cry? Do different kinds of crying. So, describe to me what are some different ways of crying. You all cry differently, don't you? What sort of noise do you make? Explain it to me. See if you can demonstrate what you do. What sounds do you make? (Windenhahn 1982)

To that the dancer Nazareth Panadero answered:

When I cry, I feel it in my throat; it gets big, and my breath sticks there. Later my head gets big, and if I try to speak, my voice is lower than usual. If someone is there, I try to laugh a bit. And when I see people, I try to keep my face quite still and my throat too. Everything is closed, and the tears come down. (Windenhahn 1982)

The other dancers followed with their descriptions. When Jan Minarik refused to answer, saying that he had cried the previous night and did not want to relive it or to make up a response, Bausch replied:

It is not a matter of pretending. I didn't ask you to go there and cry. I asked you to try to think about what happens when you cry, the sounds....I didn't ask you why you cry, or when was the last time you cried. I asked "How do people cry?" (Windenhahn 1982)

Instead of asking the dancers to cry, simulating real experiences, Bausch asked them to describe the experience when it did happen. By doing so, she transformed the past experiences into symbolic form.

Dance grows out of symbolic reconstruction rather than from "spontaneous" or "direct" expression.

This method used by Bausch (figure 3) is even clearer in a later rehearsal for the same piece, when she asked the members of the company to describe how they laughed while dancing in couples:

> But you must remain perfectly serious. I want to hear not how you laugh, but how you laugh*ed*, how you used to laugh in the past. There is not very much to laugh nowadays....You don't have to tell us the reason, only how. (Windenhahn 1982)

Following the improvisations of Jan Minarik and Meryl Tankard, Bausch pointed out that at the end of the skit, they were not being true to the desired intention of the exercise, and were laughing instead of describing the laughter. In this initial phase of the creative process, Bausch was concerned not with the expression of present experiences but with the translation of past experiences into symbolic language.

In the piece *A Game of Sadness* (*Ein Trauerspiel*, 1993), Bausch asked for "something that makes you very, very happy" (Amarante, appendix A). In response, Ruth Amarante created an improvisation in which she runs and dives into a bucket—representing her pleasant feelings of diving into the sea. Bausch selected Amarante's scene without dwelling on its personal signification. The original experience (meaning) is only relevant as an aesthetically reconstructed memory. In fact, in this initial phase, performance brings past experiences as the absence of present experience. Only later in the process do different experiences and meanings emerge from symbolic language.

After Bausch selects some scenes from this improvisation phase, the dancers "spend a long time just repeating improvisations. From these she further chooses" (appendix A). Bausch intervenes during the dancers' repetitions, altering the "original" improvisation. According to Amarante, "from all the improvisations—hundreds of them—she chooses one person's improvisation and asks this person to perform it in different ways. Sometimes she chooses specific improvisations from one person, but only fragments of them. She changes things a little" (appendix A). Through fragmentation and repetition, the personal histories and the feeling they evoke are increasingly transformed and dissociated from the dancers' personality and re-shaped into an aesthetic form.

Figure 3. Pina Bausch
© Photo by Euler Paixão

Approximately every four days during the improvisations, Bausch introduces two or more small movements to be learned and explored by the dancers. She then asks each of the dancers to join these small movements with some of the pre-selected personal improvisations, culminating in the composition of a solo dance. As reported by Amarante, some of the solos created by the dancers may or may not be repetitive in various degrees. However, it is Bausch's direction that makes them clearly repetitive to the audience: "In general, when the repetition is so obviously noticed by the public, then it is Pina's repetition....In the new piece [*A Game of Sadness*], I lean my body against the wall; this was the only thing I did in the improvisation—I am 'glued' to the wall" (Amarante, appendix A). During rehearsals, Bausch asked Amarante to repeat this improvisation several times, and this repetitive version became part of the piece. As described by Amarante, such intervention into her initial improvisation provoked changes in her original feelings while performing it:

> In the new piece, I have to do this in the second act for twenty minutes, all the time....It is totally crazy. It starts fine; it is a good sensation. But then it ends up being quite depressing; even for those who are just watching from the outside—a person that is there all the time, beating herself against the wall, falling down, and standing up, beating again on the wall, falling down on the floor... these are the things that she likes. Because, when we dancers repeat the movements, at least we don't stay the same person as when we started. You change as well. And she appreciates this change with the same type of movement....the movement...is loaded with possibilities and when you repeat it so many times, these possibilities grow and accumulate on each other. (appendix A)

Repetition, initially used as the reconstruction of past experiences, later provides diverse and unpredictable experiences in both performer and audience, resulting in increased possibilities for interpretation.

At the end of the process, Bausch suggests specific combinations to each dancer: "try to put together this with this, this with that; try to do this with this other person" (appendix A). Onstage, the dancers repeat their stories several times within these different combinations of scenes. As Bausch explains it:

> There is nothing there to start with. There are only answers: sentences, little scenes someone's shown you. It's all separate to start with. Then at a certain

point I'll take something which I think is right and join it to something else. This with that, that with something else. One thing with various other things. And by the time I've found the next thing I think is right, then the little thing I had is already a lot bigger. And then I go off in a completely different direction. It starts really small and gets gradually bigger. (in Servos and Weigelt 1984, 235–236)

Thus, the pieces include different artistic means in a balance between the dancers' and Bausch's creation. She guides the dancers' manipulation and transformation of their histories. And this aesthetic experimentation might continue when the piece is already being performed on stage. As recounted by Amarante:

It can happen as it did in *Ein Trauerspiel*. During the second act there were several different songs, and then on the day of the dress rehearsal she took them all out and put in Schubert's *Winterreise*. It was a shock for everybody. Nobody knows what may happen. During the time onstage, the first days, the first weeks, she still continues to change it. (appendix A)

A separation does not necessarily occur between creative process and final product—both being marked by the repetition and transformation of the dancers' personal histories. The pieces are constantly in process.

In general, stage performances that are presented more than once necessarily deal with repetition. On each night, a group supposedly repeats the same piece, which is necessarily another performance since it takes place at another moment. This paradox of being different while repeating itself is intrinsic to the nature of the performing arts (Phelan 1993). Bausch's works are not simply included in this paradox, but they critically include it. She questions dance's inherently repetitive nature in order to create a constantly transforming composition.

In November 1994, I watched the performance of *Two Cigarettes in the Dark* (1985) five times in the same week. There was definitely a basic structure for the piece, and many detailed gestures were just the same. But many differences also occurred from night to night. Actions took place in different places onstage, or a little later or earlier, provoking a new composition of scenes. I could understand how each night could invoke different perceptions and reactions by the audience.

Some of the actions by their nature were improvisational. In the second act, Jakob Andersen tries to keep his balance while standing on a rolling log. Andersen's action was planned, to an extent, but the dynamics of his weight over the tree trunk varied from night to night, creating different movements. On the third night, he fell off the log. Yet his fall did not look like a mistake at all but part of his performance. Andersen's dance sequence is not his successful balancing on the log, but his attempt at it.

I also had the opportunity to watch *Kontakthof* (1978) and *1980—A Piece by Pina Bausch* (*1980—Ein Stück von Pina Bausch*) twice, each separated by more than ten years. In both pieces, the combinations and sequencing of scenes had noticeably changed over time. The company's repertory is in a constant process of repetition and transformation. The performance of pieces ten years after their premier offers further transformation of the original histories. The original scenes, based on the dancers' personal histories, are probably performed by different dancers years later. The scenes, already transformed during their repetitions in the creative process, are learned later through repetition by other dancers. A new dancer initially learns the scene's movements, words, and sounds. Only after learning these formal elements, associations and feelings are evoked in the new dancer.

In the 1984 performance of *1980* at the Sadler's Wells Theatre, London, Anne Marie Benati stands on a chair and tells the audience about the times her father dressed her as a child. He would put her on a chair, comb her hair with difficulty, put on her dress, and forgetting an important detail—"...and then we both laugh like crazy because you can't go to the streets without underwear." In the performance, a male dancer acts out the actions of her father as she describes each detail, trying to repeat the scene with perfect accuracy. In the 1994 performance of *1980* at the Wuppertal Opera House, Amarante took over Benati's role, and did it with astonishing similarity (I refer back to a video of the 1984 performance of the piece when comparing it to the 1994 performance). It was not at all apparent that it wasn't Amarante's history. When asked about this, Amarante replied:

> In the beginning it was hard, but now I am starting to find this little girl....It is her [Benati's] history, but I take it for myself. So, it is as if it were mine. My father died a long time ago, too, so it is very related with the loss of a close, dear person [as for Benati]. (appendix A)

Benati's aesthetic reconstruction of her personal history evoked Amarante's personal history, instigating a constant dialogue between form and meaning at simultaneously personal and interpersonal levels.

In fact, such is the structure of any representation: someone's story is transformed into an aesthetic form that is performed by different dancers or actors. Bausch's works not only tell someone's story. They also tell the story of learning to perform personal and social stories (such as Benati's dressing habits with her father). Bausch's pieces re-present the structure of re-presentation. Her dancers do not learn and perform new roles as another layer of movement vocabulary. Instead, they learn and perform the personal and social process of learning and performing in both life and theater. Through such a re-presentation, they question and transform the movement vocabularies layered on their bodies.

The company's stage scenes develop out of the repetition and transformation of physical, social, cultural, and emotional repertory. This structural quality is carried along into stage performance, affecting both dancers and audience. Onstage, as in the creative process, repetition initially provokes personal separation from the created form, and only later does it create meanings out of the form. A narrative may be initially established by each scene, but it is soon to be broken and changed by the insistent repetition of the scenes. This fragmentation breaks the audience's expectations of a linear and resolving narrative, disappointing and distancing the public from the action onstage.

When I first watched Benati's childhood scene in *1980*, I was immediately captured by its form, and associated a meaning to it. Gradually, her descriptive attitude confounded me. Her words and performance were obviously a stage reconstruction and not the real fact, but they evoked an actual moment—one that was however out of reach. The scene's meaning was actually evoked by the absence of the dancer's feelings as experienced in the past. The constant dialogue between these two major forces—the scene's obvious fakeness, and its deep echo of absence—finally took me into a third force: the actual stage performance, the gestures, sounds, the scene's visual impact. I then began to experience the scene according to my own histories.

When watching the scene performed by Amarante, any previous perceptions were intensified. I knew the story was not originally Amarante's history; so I was quite skeptical about its meaning. But she performed it with such confidence that I found myself being drawn into the performance, leaving me with mixed feelings about its authenticity. The scene mesmerized me once more, and I got to experience its form with my new feelings and interpretations.

The de-identification provoked by repetition in both dancers and viewers empowers and frees up physical, social, cultural, and emotional repertories. Other transitory meanings re-emerge out of these repertories in another sensory and psychic levels for both performers and audience. In most theatrical dancing, the audience is a passive viewer who witnesses intangible bodies showing their abilities and talents. Bausch's dances, on the other hand, capture and transform the audience's expectations of the dance, evoking their constant questioning of their own role as a viewer. As interpreted by Norbert Servos and Gert Weigelt, "It is only during this process of (active) reception that the artwork becomes coherent and complete. The viewer is no longer the consumer of inconsequential pleasures, nor is he witness to an interpretation of reality. He is involved and included in a sensual [and mutating] experience of reality" (1984, 21). And as described by Pina Bausch:

> It is never how it really happened; it always transforms itself many and many times, into something that ends up belonging to all of us. If something is true in one person, and he or she tells something about his or her feelings, I think we end up recognizing the feeling, it is not a private history. We talk about something that we all have. We all know these feelings and have them together. (in Durán, 1994)

3
BETWEEN ARTIFICIALITY AND EXPERIENCE: THE RE-PRESENTED GESTURE

And then I'll know to paint and write, after the strange but intimate answer. Listen to me, listen to the silence. What I tell you is never what I tell you but something else. Capture this thing that escapes me, and I nonetheless live off of it and am on the surface of brilliant darkness. One instant takes me unthinkingly to the next, and the athematic theme keeps unfolding without a plan yet geometrically, like the successive figures in a kaleidoscope.
      Clarice Lispector (1989)

Dance, with or without the formal repetition of movements, is repetitive as part of the Symbolic order: "Now, a human gesture does belong with language and not with motor manifestations" (Lacan 1988, 255). In the signifying chain, performed movements open up the choices of their interpretation, freeing themselves from final and clear meanings. Nonetheless, in many technical dance forms, repetition is used as a compositional tool, to construct an abstract narrative conveying themes chosen by the choreographer.

In Bausch's works, repetition is used as dance's self-reflexive tool: repetition explores the repetitive nature of the Symbolic order. By repeating a movement sequence several times, dance's inherently linguistic repetitive nature becomes reflected in the dance's composition. Dance is not helplessly included in the signifying chain, trying to convey a meaning external to it. Through movement repetition, dance actively works through language, formally incorporating and exploring the power of the Symbolic order over "motor manifestations." As its own subject, dance recreates body meanings. Between artificiality and experience (Vaccarino 1993), dance constantly questions and redefines itself as an art form.

The exact repetition of a movement sequence—"obsessive" repetition—dismantles the convention of dance as a spontaneous expression. This is particularly relevant in Bausch's use of daily reactions and gestures in solo scenes. Movements pertaining to dance technique vocabulary are more easily seen as an abstraction, different from spontaneous expression. Yet, everyday reactions and gestures are more easily seen as spontaneous, momentary response to a present event. The staging of daily reactions gives dance the impression of being more spontaneous than if technical movements were staged. However, Bausch stages precisely what is usually associated with spontaneous response in order to expose its artificiality in both life and theater.

In *Arien* (1979), repetition transforms the audience's perception of a daily spontaneous reaction such as laughter. In the piece, a hippopotamus (prop) comes on stage unnoticed by the dancers, but having already surprised the audience. Soon after, Josephine Ann Endicott finds herself alone onstage with the animal. She laughs continuously, looking at it between bursts of laughter, and leaves the stage guiding it out. Endicott's first burst of laughter appears convincing, for it expresses her surprise at facing such an unexpected event. But as soon as she keeps repeating the same reaction, it loses its power as a messenger from her "inner sensations," and refers back to itself as signs escaping from a meaningful essence. The reaction's absence of meaning, its absurdness, becomes its meaning. The laughter conveys falseness, in both dance and everyday life. The public is again surprised, seeing its own initial reaction (laughter) being incorporated and distorted onstage.

In another piece, the dancer's surprise is included in the mode of repetition, dismantling even further the myth of authentic inner sensations and their spontaneous expression in daily reactions and gestures. In a scene of *1980—A Piece by Pina Bausch* (*1980—Ein Stück von Pina Bausch*), Mechthild Grossmann's costume and attitude contrast with those of the other female dancers onstage. While the other female dancers wear long formal silk dresses and tight hair, Grossmann wears a large and wide green leather coat and translucent black stockings; she has one front tooth painted black, and her hair is loose and wild, constantly falling over her face. Her wide and aggressive body attitude also differs from the polite chatting among the dancers in the background.

Walking around the stage with her head and shoulders advanced forward and her legs opened to the sides, Grossmann opens her arms in sudden jerky movements while emphatically laughing and screaming "fantastic" several times in reference to different objects and people in the theater. For instance, she repeats her actions in reference to the stage set design, to the dancers, and to some audience members. This repetition is slightly different from that of Endicott, as Grossmann identically reacts to different situations—confirming her artificiality toward both objects and people.

The scene also upsets conventions of dance as abstract movement and of theater as role-playing. Here, dancers represent social characters instead of performing abstract movements. They remind us that dance is re-presentation. Although quite verbal, Grossmann's performance is largely supported by her body movement and attitude: theater gains a strong dance component.

Just as repetition demystifies dances as a spontaneous expression, it also provokes experience. In *1980*, when Anne Marie Benati "run[s] round the room fifty times calling out 'I'm tired,'" she finally gets really tired (Wright 1989, 116). Her movements, initially light and full of energy, gradually become slower, her weight more and more relaxed at each step, as if her limbs were becoming heavier by increasing passive weight; her breathing becomes intensified, and she can barely speak in the same tempo as before. The artificiality of the initial re-presentation, speaking what she was not feeling, becomes a real experience through mechanical repetition. Now that she really feels tired, she can hardly speak or dance, expressing a continuous challenge between art and experience.

Re-presentation provokes experience and also extinguishes it. In a moment from *On the Mountain a Cry Was Heard* (*Auf dem Gebirge hat man ein Geschrei gehört*, 1984), even exhaustion is swallowed by repetition. This happens when Josephine Ann Endicott repeats a small upper body sequence while running alone in a circle onstage. The scene starts with Endicott coming on stage already performing the sequence. It is a continuous repetitive scene, with the sequences flowing naturally from one to the other.

Her movements are light and free flowing, with slight alteration of timing, and with independence between running and the circular movements of her arms. With both arms semi-flexed and close to her trunk, her right hand rotates around the left hand, describing a curve in space toward her left side. Then her right hand brings her rotating left hand to the right shoulder, where it reposes. Soon the right hand goes to the left shoulder, and for one instant both arms are crossed over her chest. The hands soon fall from her shoulders, and with the arms flexed, her upper trunk and head curve slightly forward and down in a concave shape. From within this shape, the right hand rotates around the left hand, and the sequence restarts.

Endicott repeats the upper body sequence at least four times at each completed circle. By her fifth round, her arms extend almost entirely during the shaping of the hands. The sequence becomes slower, and the movements become heavier, mainly in her legs, and less precise due to increasing free flow and its supporting shape flow. She seems to be tired and cannot perform as she did earlier. Then she suddenly falls backward onto the floor and stays there breathing heavily. She suddenly sits up, facing the audience, with her legs straight, spine erect, and arms by her side. Then she drops her knees to her side, stands forward-and-up, and restarts her sequence.

This time around, right before falling, her arms tend to extend to the left side when shaping, rather than staying flexed and close to the trunk as at the beginning of the scene. Now, when curving the torso slightly forward and down, she almost falls to her right, hovering over the floor (right low), but then continues running and performing the upper body sequence. Suddenly she falls again, lies down, rests, sits up, and gets up as in the first time. She restarts her sequence, which has similar qualities to those performed in the beginning of the scene, but with gradually fewer changes. The little rest seems to provide her the recuperation she needs to perform as before. Even experience (physical exhaustion) and an eventual change (rest) became part of the repetitive sequence. When incorporated into the sequence, the change was precisely what prevented further changes. Nothing is immune to repetition.

By exploring its own linguistic means, dance is able to simultaneously convey themes of social relevance. In Bausch's works, the group of dancers creates a formal composition and constitutes a metaphor for society. The long lines of dancers repeating the same sequence in unison overpowers personal expression, portraying society as mechanical. In the first scene of *1980*, twelve well-dressed dancers walk in line through the aisles of the theater while performing a little arm sequence in unison over and over again to the sound of a cabaret song. They look and smile at the audience in a childlike, playful manner, while their hands and forearms describe circular forms in space like the contours of an exaggeratedly rounded body. The dancers' attitude is almost cynical, associating childlike lightness with elegant and sophisticated movements while invading the space of the audience. The public is hypnotized and confused by the intimacy of the dancers' smiles, gaze, and beautiful gestures that are so close and strangely mechanical.

Such group repetition places both dance and society within the Symbolic (Lacan), as chains of signifiers. In the same scene, contrasting to the group repetition, a couple dances slowly and close together on upstage right. Within the signifying chain, the spontaneity and mechanization are not antagonistic but co-exist and intervene with each other.

The contrast between social mechanization and personal life is questioned by repetition in *Arien*. In the last part of the piece, as if following orders, all dancers run continuously back-and-forth from upstage to downstage. Alternately, the dancers then collapse and restart. As with Josephine Ann Endicott in *1980*, exhaustion becomes part of the repetitive sequence, though it is now in a group composition. At one point, total exhaustion is apparent and dancers gradually stop and gather at upstage as if posing for a picture, except one dancer—Endicott—who continues alone, performing the same back-and-forth running.

Individuality emerged not as personal expression but from the social mechanization. In *Arien*, Endicott's originality resides in being even more compulsive than the others. Repetition breaks through the dichotomy between individual authenticity and social mechanization. Neither individual nor society is posited as spontaneous: Endicott repeats an imposed movement pattern, while the group artificially poses for a replication (photograph) of their present performance.

The Temporal and Visual Nature of Dance

Even in Camus—this love for heroism. So there isn't another way? No, even to understand is already heroism. So one man cannot simply open one door and look?
    Clarice Lispector (1992)

I never thought: "That's how it is."...I often thought of something completely different, meant something different—but not only that....You can see it like this or like that. It just depends on the way you watch. But single-stranded thinking that they interpret into it simply isn't right....You can always watch the other way.
    Pina Bausch (quoted in Hoghe, 1980)

In Bausch's works, repetition creates self-reflexive signs that explore dance's temporal and visual means. In *Mountain,* the stage is covered with earth. In one scene, Beatrice Libonati uses the same motions to dig holes in different parts of the upstage area. When digging the first hole, her repetitive actions seem to have the function of making the hole deeper. But she soon moves to another spot, another, and another, establishing a routine in which her movements do not have an obvious practical function. In the scene, "[r]epetition stalls time, or keeps it in a perpetual present" (Goldberg 1989, 115). Yet, it gradually creates a sense of time progression, because the hole being dug in the present looks like the prior one, though it is necessarily another one. The scene then becomes a constant and unsuccessful attempt to preserve the present moment. As in the signifying chain, "when the signified [present moment] seems finally to be within reach, it dissolves at the explorer's touch into yet more signifiers" (Bowie 1991, 64). Through repetition, dance articulates its inherent ephemeral quality.

In another scene in the same piece, Libonati stands still on center stage singing in low voice with her eyes closed. In a repetitive action, Jakob Andersen puts white chalk over Libonati's hair with attention, care, and constant timing. Gradually, Libonati's hair turns white, as if getting older with each of Andersen's gestures. Years of life are concentrated in those minutes of repetition. Here repetition neither "stalls [performance] time," nor establishes present time as a constant loss. Instead, it establishes time as a progression in both performance and life.

While the white-haired Libonati stands alone on center stage with her eyes closed, Jan Minarik comes onstage and announces: "Intermission." The audience starts an effusive applause, but gradually stops due to Libonati's persistent stillness on center stage. As the music stops, Libonati's silence is invaded by the audience's tumultuous voices as it begins leaving the theater. One viewer asks: "Is it all right if I stand up right now?" It is embarrassing to leave while dancers are still "re-presenting," but the intermission was announced! The contradiction expands the re-presentation: there is no intermission in the progression of human life. Throughout intermission, Libonati stays onstage with tears rolling down from her eyes. When she finally leaves the stage during the beginning of the second act, she receives a great deal of applause from the audience.

Bausch's works are usually three to four hours long. Her performances do not concentrate daily or "real" time into a representative capsule. Events happen in "real" time and are not rushed or compacted. The audience has time to absorb the material presented onstage, to be taken by it, or even to get bored. The long lengths and the repetitive scenes of the works push the audience to its limit, provoking an unusual experience.

As a member of the audience, I have personally experienced exhaustion during many of her pieces. In the first hour of long performances, I am usually intellectually aware of the stage happenings. As time progresses, I start becoming tired, and my body relaxes into the seat. I become less judgmental and more open to surprising experiences at emotional and physical levels. The constant transformation of the repeated scenes provokes an interplay between old and new images/concepts within my own—now more susceptible—perceptions.

The repetition of a movement phrase impresses the images in the viewer's memory, providing new ways of seeing dance. In the beginning of *Mountain*, Minarik is onstage, his big broad body covered with a bathing suit, cap, swimming goggles and nose protector, plastic surgical gloves, and biker's professional sneakers. He looks down at his hands with constant and slow timing. The right hand slightly opens the bathing suit, and the left one pulls out an empty balloon as if it were his sexual organ. Keeping the same rhythm, he brings the balloon to his mouth, and inflates it with repetitive and slow exhalations till it bursts. The audience cannot see Minarik's face, only the growing balloon, Minarik's arms, and his massive trunk and legs. He repeats this sequence a few times. The sudden explosion of the balloons is the only break to the monotonous timing of Minarik's movements. But even such a surprise becomes monotonous and predictable after the second repetition.

In the beginning, the action can be associated with successive erections, and the audience laughs effusively at the first two times. They then become quiet at this strange and repetitive scene that has no other background movement or sound. However, during the third repetition, I noticed his massive torso bulging and hollowing, widening and narrowing, lengthening and shortening at each inhalation and exhalation. This struck me as amazing in the middle of that apparent routine.

Instead of symbolic allusions and gestures, I was faced with a crucial bodily function intensified by mechanization. Repetition initially dismantles dance as spontaneous expression, positing it as part of the Symbolic. It then allows a temporary opening of the Symbolic order into the Real—"motor manifestations" and experience.

Minarik's scene repeats itself in other contexts with subtle changes, in a form of "altered" repetition. In the next scene, the dancer comes back on stage, behaving as the same character, but now carrying lots of inflated and colorful balloons. He comes to the same spot on the stage and throws the balloons on the floor. He begins to again inflate balloons from his bathing suit, but this time without exploding them. This time, he throws these also on the floor. At this point, Francis Viet picks up the inflated balloons from the floor and places them under the thin and delicate body of Jakob Andersen that is stretched out on the floor. Objects destroyed in the first scene by a hulking physical presence, now protect a fragile frame. Surprised, the audience watches previously exploded objects become delicately functional.

Viet and Andersen then leave the stage, and Minarik stops the inflation and stares at the audience. In his constant and slow timing, he walks slightly forward toward an inflated balloon. He sits on it and in a sudden, strong, and direct attack, explodes it; he pauses while sitting on the floor, and looks at the audience. Minarik re-enacts his destructive compulsion of the first scene, now by repeatedly sitting on inflated balloons and exploding them. The scene sets up a regularity of behavior, allowing us to see it in its details. Its structure is repeated with an unexpected, subtle, but relevant change. This way, Bausch (de)constructs ways of dancing and watching dance.

In "intermittent" repetitions, the same action is repeated in different contexts of the same piece, also exploring the audience's visual perception. In *1980*, Nazareth Panadero drinks tea onstage while two other dancers also serve it to the audience. The audience joins the dancer in the physical experience of this social act. Later in the same piece, Lutz Förster and Mechthild Grossmann drink tea together as a typical British couple, sighing to each other: "Oh...Dear...Could you please pass the sugar?"

After a while, two other events that were previously performed separately invade the polite atmosphere. Jan Minarik, with a nylon stocking covering his head, enacts a murder with a gun. Meryl Tankard screams hysterically while carrying a huge, loud portable stereo around the stage. Her disruptive behavior has no effect on the polite British couple, who continue to sip their tea as if nothing was happening. The overlapping of the three events changes the viewers' perception and interpretation of the earlier tea scene. It now shows the hysterical and destructive nature of seemingly polite and respectful social interaction. Repetition multiplies and accumulates meanings, legitimating dance as a medium for social criticism:

> Dance theatre has developed into such an archeology of ways of life. Gesture, movement and space are elements of an aesthetic of crossing boundaries, which seeks to develop a new way of perceiving in opposition to ready-made worlds of images which tamper with our ways of seeing. (Baxmann 1990, 60)

Tracing Social Significance

Dance and society are equally permeated and defined by the Symbolic. Therefore, by exploring itself as language, dance explores social relationships. In *Kontakthof* (1978), the whole group of well-dressed dancers performs a short sequence over and over again to the sound of a repetitive cabaret song. While performing the sequence, they gradually approach downstage with a fixed mincing gaze at the audience. Their precise and fragmented movements seem an exaggeration of a crippled person's walking pattern.

Although the dancers look straight at the audience, their advance is not in a direct pathway. Throughout the sequence, they transfer their weight from left to right feet with an emphasis sideways rather than forward. To arrive downstage, they have to do the sequence innumerable times. In midst of the innumerous side steps, they advance slightly forward only when moving like a cripple by kicking one hip forward. Common knowledge would indicate that such highly trained ballet dancers are capable of moving in the most elegant manner. Nonetheless, they seem to have a dislocated hip joint when moving toward the audience.

The threatening attitude of the dancers resides not only in their direct gaze while approaching the audience, but also in the sequence when they stand military-like, with legs slightly apart. The scene could be viewed as a critical reference to early German dance in relation to the Third Reich (Preston-Dunlop 1988; Kew 1999). The group looks like a threatening advancing army, but one that is composed of crippled soldiers instead of healthy representatives of strong state power:

> This is no shapeless crowd whose edges could overflow, whose direction could change, whose eyes could wander. This is an ordered mass,...the gaze hypnotically fixed, the direction is indicated, the only one in which "the movement" will turn, straight ahead. It knows no rhythm unless it is a march; it knows no open space, unless it is occupied. One people, one empire, one "Führer," ...the yearning to unite with others as one unites and merges in love, in order to lustily transgress the restrictive boundaries of one's own loneliness? (Servos 1990, 63, 64)

In the scene from *Kontakthof,* the dancers break not only the model of physical perfection, but also the illusion of group unity and completeness. As the music ends, the dancers stop downstage, maintaining their gaze at the audience, with their faces inexpressive. The audience now has a clearer view of the dancers, who are neatly groomed in formal silk dresses and black suits. Then Anne Marie Benati gradually turns her head from side to side and begins laughing. Her movements seem like a compulsive "no" offered to the ordered group sequence.

As her movement becomes more energetic and the turns of the head bigger, the laughter becomes louder and stronger. In opposition to the group's outlook, Benati becomes increasingly uncombed, noisy, and loose in her head movement. She maintains her body still, straight, and tensely vertical, similar to the rest of the group. Her head then goes from right to left, and is loosely thrown out of its vertical axis with free flow and acceleration with no clear spatial direction. When achieving her maximum voice volume and movement speed, she slightly flexes her right leg and collapses with her body rigid and tense onto the floor.

The group turns around, begins to sing the previous repetitive melody gradually faster and louder, and repeats the little movement sequence while returning upstage. The group almost steps over Benati petrified on the floor. The same walking, now seen from backward, has quite a different impact. The pelvic kick backward exaggerates the dancers' buttocks in tight dresses and pants and jumps toward the audience in a comical attack similar to farting. The dancers walk away from both the audience and Benati in a debauching attitude (figure 4).

As they approach the dim upstage, their singing becomes more forceful, like a triumphant army march. In contrast, Benati's still, silent

Figure 4. The Wuppertal Dance Theater in *Kontakthof*
© Photo by Gert Weigelt www.gert-weigelt.de

body in highlighted downstage in her shiny white silk dress. Gradually, the group dissolves with only one dancer continuing the singing. Again, the individual is detached from the group, reinforcing Benati's sequence.

The scene can be interpreted as contrasting an expressive individual and machine-like, mechanical society, but both are equally repetitive. Laughter, normally associated with a natural expression of happiness, becomes suffocation and desperation through social pressure. Benati repeats until being able to impose her voice and fluidity, becoming the center of attention in a static and mute group that inhabits her from the neck down. However, by this process of imposing herself, she actually distorts her own movements and even seems to hurt herself by rigidly falling down. The scene does not comfort us with the illusion of completeness and group immersion. Benati is fragmented between the head (free flowing individualistic movements), and the body (group's controlled posture), in a repressive social process, exposing her inescapable solitude.

In a following scene of the same piece, Benati repeats her solo exactly in the same way but in a different context. In this scene, the dancers sit like an audience along the upstage wall, while a few of them go individually to center stage and perform a brief repetitive individual sequence. In one of these sequences, a dancer closes the upstage door three times as if on his fingers, forcefully laughing each time. In another of the sequences, Ed Kortlandt lies down on the floor, holding up an apparently heavy table and lets it fall over his belly four times, loudly laughing. Beatrice Libonati sets up four chairs on center stage and runs laughing hysterically and stumbles on the chairs. Anne Marie Benati comes on to center stage, and laughs exactly as before, finally collapsing on the floor. A man closes the piano twice as if on his fingers, laughing loudly and repetitively. Meryl Tankard laughs hysterically while running in circles, in the middle of which she attempts to throw up. Then Josephine Ann Endicott laughs hysterically while running back-and-forth on downstage, and twice throws herself against the wall. At the end of each of these individual sequences, the rest of the dancers behave like an audience by applauding the soloist effusively.

While Benati's laughter formerly expressed her desperation and stood out from the rest of the group, now it is disconnected from any emotional content and is identical to the others. They all perform something exaggerated and attention-calling, hurting themselves while laughing loudly and repeatedly, with the explicit intention of receiving the other dancers' attention and applause. The concept of authenticity as a vigorous emotional expression—previously posited by Benati's screams within the mechanical group—is dismantled. Dance as spontaneous, real experience, is substituted by dance as re-presentation and self-wounding to receive the group's recognition and reward.

The scene unsettles the concept of dance as spontaneous expression, non-mediated by language. The scene also questions the general notion of pain as an authentic, real experience, prior to language's translation:

> Whatever pain achieves, it achieves in part through its unsharability, and it ensures this unsharability through its resistance to language....Physical pain does not simply resist language but actively destroys it, bringing about an immediate reversion to a state anterior to language, to the sounds and cries a human being makes before language is learned....Contemporary philosophers have habituated us to the recognition that our interior states of consciousness are regularly accompanied by objects in the external world, that we do not simply "have feelings" but have feelings *for* somebody or something...physical pain—unlike any other state of consciousness—has no referential content. It is not *of* or *for* anything. It is precisely because it takes no object that it, more than any other phenomenon, resists objectification in language. (Scarry 1985, 4–5)

In the previously described scene, pain is produced by symbolic language—the represented gestures—and its repetition, artificially produced for the audience. The expected "sounds and cries...before language is learned" of the dancers in pain is substituted by a common daily reaction—laughter—repeated to the point of exaggeration and artificiality. Repetition in Bausch's works disturbs the conventions of independent and isolated "interior states of consciousness." Her works suggest that individual feelings are determined by language and repetition within social relationships of power.

By applauding themselves, the group of dancers re-presents the audience's role, taking on its power. The dancers do not need the audience's applause: They can applaud themselves. The power relationship between audience and performer becomes dance's subject. Stage performance reveals dance as physical self-aggression in order to gain the audience's applause. Social and theatrical roles are equally questioned within sado-masochistic and repetitive attention-seeking context. Not only dance gesture, but dancers, audience members, and society also became included in a signifying chain marked by the inexhaustible search for meaning—in this case, the others' attention and recognition. In this context, repetition establishes a chain in which dichotomies, such as individual and society, authentic and mechanical, dancers and audience, and art and life, become overlapped and intertwined, challenging and transforming each other.

Benati's sequence is repeated again in a later scene of *Kontakthof*. At the beginning of the scene, all the dancers are seated on chairs along the upstage wall, arms crossed linked in a chain, swinging side to side in tempo to the waltz. Josephine Ann Endicott uncrosses her arms and runs toward the more illuminated downstage. There she starts a sequence marked by free flow, light weight, acceleration to deceleration, circular shapes and designs, especially with the arms. She ends the sequence at downstage right and pauses.

Jan Minarik carefully approaches Endicott from behind, and he slowly touches her shoulders lightly. She then immediately restarts a sequence of self-caressing. This is a quicker version of a previous sequence from a section where each dancer performed individualized self-caressing sequences (see chapter 4, "Women and Men"). Endicott touches different parts of her upper body, as if trying to feel them. Then she runs back to stage left followed by Minarik and pauses again.

Minarik touches Endicott's shoulders again and she falls down, rolls to her sides, stands up toward the audience, and restarts the sequence of the free-flowing circular shapes in the same spot as before. This time, Minarik touches her waist in the middle of her sequence, hastening its end and prompting Endicott to run downstage right and re-perform her self-caressing sequence. Minarik follows Endicott, who this time falls down even before he touches her. This time, the sequences of self-caressing, falls, and circular shapes are mixed together, and Minarik gets included in them.

This reinforces and overlaps Endicott's quick and fluid escapes from Minarik left to right across the front of the stage. At the same time, Dominique Mercy and Meryl Tankard enter euphorically dancing to the pompous waltz with Tankard touching Mercy's face (just as she did some scenes previously to her own face in her self-caressing sequence). As with Endicott's repetition, Tankard increases speed and tension, and the original dance gradually changes. Mercy continues his steps, moving and turning by himself, while Tankard tries to catch and touch him. As the music becomes faster and more intense, the two stage couples look similar, but with reversed gender roles. Minarik runs after Endicott, trying to touch her, while she wants to dance by herself; Tankard runs after Mercy, trying to touch him, while he wants to dance alone.

In the meantime, another couple interacts onstage. Silvia Kesselheim and a male dancer come onstage and perform a sequence done earlier by the whole group of dancers. She brings on a chair, sits on it in profile to the audience, while the man stands in front of her. Then he insistently tries to touch different spots of her body, with sharp, fast arm movements. Kesselheim repeatedly performs a set of defensive body positions on the chair, quickly going forward and sideways.

While these three couples perform onstage, with the group in unison in the background, Benati leaves her chair and comes center stage. She then performs her laughing sequence and falls exactly as in the two previous episodes of the piece. But this time the audience cannot hear her laughter because the music is extremely loud. As Benati's head movements become increasingly intense, the music achieves its climax, followed by a short, silent pause. At this moment, Benati falls down to her side, and the couples stop running and stand close to each other with exalted breathing while the group of dancers stops swinging. All remain still, until Benati stands up and slowly walks back to her chair. The couples gradually do the same in slow tempo. For a few minutes, the stage stays dim and silent.

As in the first two scenes it was previously presented, Benati's sequence here is different from anything else on stage. However, this time it is not opposed (as in the first scene), or similar (as in the second scene) to the other stage events. This time, Benati's difference centralizes all the divergent forces in the scene, in an intense moment followed by a sober and quiet one. Once Benati's laughter in not heard as it was previously in the two other times, her movements are dissociated from her voice, instead, they become associated with the music in synchrony with the other stage events. This synchrony allows Benati to suddenly take control over the other stage happenings and become the scene's central figure. Her sequence, initially implying difference and alienation from the group, now connects individuals, couples, and group within repetitive relationships.

The repetition of Benati in three different contexts transformed it in a connecting signifying chain from which other imports eventually emerged. Initially, the scene conveyed meanings associated with society and its individuals. After all those repetitions, Benati's desperate laughter became independent and strong signifiers; her laughter, later drowned by an overpowering music, communicated a human condition within the Symbolic. Just as the muted laughter's desperation—a metaphor for the desperation of Benati, the couples, the group of dancers, the audience, and humanity within the chain—seemed to resonate onstage. Suddenly Benati's sequence gained a totally different and much more powerful meaning than before. It was necessary for this scene to go through all these different contexts to break down presupposed interpretations and then accumulate more meanings than ever. Meaning has emerged not as a fixed concept separated from, prior to, or hidden within its form. It is instead a transitory signification about and part of the chain as much as movements, words, individuals, and society:

> [I]t is not the return of...a [platonic] supreme truth, coming to us from the beyond. It is something that comes to us from the structural necessities, something humble, born at the level of the lowest encounters and of all the talking crowd that precedes us, at the level of the structure of the signifier, of the languages spoken in a stuttering, stumbling way…. (Lacan 1978, 47)

In Bausch's works, repetition exposes and explores the chain that permeates, hinders, distorts, and determines experience and meaning in dance and social relationships. Through repetition, the audience's preconceptions of both dance and society are confirmed, twisted, and dismantled. Paradoxically, repetition opens new and unexpected ways of perceiving in performance and everyday life. This awareness of daily human relationships is a main concern for Bausch:

> What I do—watch….Perhaps that's it. The only thing I did all the time was watching people. I have only seen human relations or I have tried to see them and talk about them. That's what I am interested in. I don't know anything more important. (in Hoghe, 1980)

4

REPETITIVE BONDS OF POWER: TORTURE, VALUE, AND NEEDS OF THE BODY

What I write you is not comfortable. I'm not sharing confidences. First, I steel myself....And walking in complete darkness in search of ourselves is what we do. It hurts. But it's labor pain: something is being born that is. It is itself. It's hard like a dry stone. But the core is "it," soft and alive, perishable, in danger.
Clarice Lispector (1989)

As in the Latin proverb, *Repetitio mater lectionis*, repetition is the mother of apprenticeship. Any social learning process, including ballet training, requires discipline based on cycles of repetition that are regulated by a timetable. Through repetitive discipline, social forms gradually permeate and overpower individual ways of perception and expression. Through repetition, bodies are disciplined and controlled, becoming economically utile and productive (Foucault 1995). Paradoxically, Bausch uses such "educational" method to invert its effects, providing new ways of perceiving and expressing human relationships and the power implicit in them.

In Bausch's works, repetition dismantles the conventions of dance as spontaneous expression as well as a final stage product. She exposes dance to be a symbolic language that has been imposed on the dancers' bodies through a coercive disciplinary method present in conventional dance training and performance. In her works, the repetitive memorization of movement sequences, the dancers' life-long body training and dance's commercial implications, usually taken as part of the preparation for dance performance, become dance's subject onstage. Instead of being considered as a final and perfect product, dance becomes the exposition of its technical processes and imperfections. Dance also includes its commercial value as a power relationship between dancers and audience.

As repetition explores and unsettles conventional ways of seeing and expressing dance, the body gradually emerges as the consistent subject. It resonates as the final victim, the site of the registered coercion and pain within both theatrical and social relationships. Through repetition, dance was first dissociated from spontaneous expression, then posited as Symbolic, and is now evoked as physical within this domain. Through repetition, dance evokes its most essential means—the physical body—as an object under aesthetic and social disciplinary control. Dance becomes a critique to its own definition as the presentation of "beautiful" movements onstage. Dance's "beauty" is constantly redefined within a critical exploration of its inherent power relationships.

Dance Rehearsals

In many of the scenes in Bausch's pieces, repetition reveals dance's rehearsal process. Frequently, an isolated dancer almost invisible behind the downstage actions repeats a specific movement sequence upstage, as if trying to memorize it. The choreography becomes the dancer's *learning* of a movement combination, rather than its perfect performance. In *Kontakthof* (1978), Josephine Ann Endicott walks toward downstage center, casually eating an apple, and with her mouth half full, asks Jean-François Duroure: "Jean, come here. Can you show me that step we learned in Wuppertal?" Standing with his body facing the audience, Duroure moves his pelvis, describing half a circle along the horizontal plane. Endicott interrupts him: "Wait a minute, pull your jacket up. I can't see anything!" He lifts his suit holding it up, and looks down at his pelvis and pants. He passively follows Endicott's order, and appears to be showing a product on sale. She replies: "Good."

Endicott stands behind and to the side of Duroure, wearing a long red dress and high heels, with her long hair out. She has her hands on her hips and legs a little apart, with her weight on one foot. She seems like an arrogant, domineering dance critic observing him perform the requested movement. With both knees slightly bent, he circles his pelvis, giving quick and sharp kicks at the end of each cycle, forward, right forward middle, and left forward middle. As he kicks his pelvis forward, his flexed knees go a little further from each other, and his head and shoulders curve slightly forward.

Then, Endicott orders: "Turn around." Duroure stops the sequence and looks at her, hesitating. She gestures impatiently with her arm, indicating the direction he should turn. He turns his back to the audience, still holding his suit up and repeats the sequence. As with the cripple walking scene at the beginning of the piece seen from behind (chapter 3), Duroure's movements provoke an interesting effect. The scene is comical, and the audience laughs heartily as his buttocks stick out repeated times toward the audience in such quick tempo. Suddenly, Endicott screams: "It's not right. It's not right at all! Look." She demonstrates the movements with her arms, irritably pointing the "correct" directions of the circles, emphasizing their roundness, while saying: "Here circles, circles, circles." Her movements are bigger and more rounded circles than Duroure's. And she continues: "You are just doing this [she moves her pelvis straight from left to right]. That's not right at all."

She steps back and lets him try it again. Right before he starts, she grumbles: "Turn. Turn. The other way." He turns and faces the audience. She continues to talk as he starts the sequence: "Put your feet on the ground; and a penny, and a nickel, and a dime"; giving him some circular images he could easily associate and be stimulated by. The audience laughs loudly to Endicott's methodology, which cynically criticizes traditional ballet training. Some ballet instructors use the image of holding a coin between the buttocks in order to promote pelvic stability. And she continues to berate: "Bigger circles, bigger circles! Now, you've got a small pelvis, do it bigger so that it will look bigger. Now do it. Not so fast. Come on, do it right, I know you can do it."

In both ballet and Western culture, such pelvic movements are not part of the accepted body etiquette. Even in Brazilian culture, it is deemed provocative and taunting, and is being increasingly commercially exploited. One of the main rules in ballet, differentiating it, for example, from Modern or African dance, is its use of the pelvis as a strong and fixed stabilizer, supporting the movement of the legs and upper body. A "good" ballet dancer does not need to tilt the pelvis to be able to stretch the legs really high or jump repeated times. Contradicting this notion, in the scene the dancer's inability to tilt the pelvis makes him feel ashamed. The image of the coins is used to stimulate the mobility of this prohibited body part and associates dance with the sale of the body. In this market, the female has more ability than the man with his small pelvis. But the increasing value of the offer in coins may help him improve. In another light, Endicott's corrections could as well be associated with a woman instructing a man during lovemaking, again highlighting female dominance.

In the scene, repetition increasingly exposes movements that are culturally taboo. The audience laughs in the face of such cynical exposition. The movement is explicitly done so many times, in such an impersonal way, that its socially constructed provocative, seductive meaning is dismantled. It becomes technically routine, losing its exoticism. The audience's expectations are already unsettled by watching highly-trained ballet dancers performing such un-ballet-like movements. The audience is further jolted by witnessing an expensively produced show consisting of formally dressed dancers—"high art"—performing movements from popular culture—"low art" (Varnedoe and Gopnik 1990).

Gradually, the audience stops laughing as another revelation emerges through repetition. Endicott tells Duroure, while walking toward the group of dancers: "Keep working on it." She joins the whole group standing upstage and asks for music, calling out the sound manager's name. As in the cripple-walking scene, the whole group marches toward the audience, but now doing the circular movements of the pelvis. They do this movement over and over again to the music's tempo, as if performing a well-rehearsed sequence and at the same time "working on it." This scene blurs the distinctions between rehearsal and public performance in all the other repetitive sequences of the piece.

Exposing the repetitive method through which dancers usually learn choreography turns this method into the piece's subject, destroying the idea of a perfect, final product. Repetition is dance's theme and means. The dance work turns into a scenario for experimentation, allowing the perception and critical evaluation of the underlying structure of dance performance.

Dance Training

In many scenes of Bausch's works, repetition reveals the life-long training of the dancers and their search for perfection within competitive ballet settings. In *Bandoneon* (1980), the male dancer Dominique Mercy, dressed as a classical ballerina, attempts to perform a ballet step, but is unsuccessful and falls to the floor several times.

It was obvious that as a well-trained ballet dancer, he was capable of doing such a step. He failed in not only being able to perform the ballet step but also in the faking of his failure. Perfection and failure, as well as fakeness, became equally part of dance. The scene might also be Mercy's representation of his own history as a beginning ballet student.

Mercy's scene unsettles the social convention that learning through repetition brings perfection. He repeats because he failed and wishes to do it better next time, but he fails again and again. Mercy is caught in a chain where repetition constantly leads to failure and back to repetition, instead of gradually approaching perfection. The scene questions and reverses the notion that repetition is a successful learning method.

In some scenes, repetition exposes the social relationships within the context of classical dance's training and discipline. The interaction between individual and group can be seen in *Kontakthof*. In the second act of the piece, all of the dancers do an elegant arm sequence in unison several times while diagonally crossing the stage, looking seductively at the audience. The dancers enter and exit the stage performing the sequence like a continuous evolving chain. While elegantly walking and slightly smiling at the audience, the dancers extend their arms upward in open Vs, and suddenly and graciously drop only their wrists. Then they perform a series of elegant arm and hand gestures describing circles around the shoulders and chest areas. In a fluid movement, they raise their arms again and restart the sequence.

The dancers leave the stage from downstage right and return after a short while through upstage left. They then perform a different repetitive arm sequence in unison while walking elegantly. The continuous exit and entrance of this inexorable diagonal chain establishes a circular relationship between the stage and back stage. The fluid circular hand movements support this notion. Just as the barriers between rehearsal and performance were broken previously, dancers are now merged between stage and backstage.

In the second entrance, two dancers are introduced to the scene. Center stage, Jan Minarik acts like a ballet *maître*, observing the dancers and making notes. In the middle of the line of dancers, Monika Sagon stands out by being unable to follow the group sequence. After the first attempt, her movements become sloppy. She looks back to see what the dancer behind her is doing and misses step. She touches the top of her head instead of extending her arms up in a V, and then walks with her arms straight down while the others have them up. She suddenly jumps out of line as if expelled by the other dancers' elegant movements. She takes a few nervous steps and rejoins the line. Again she is unable to keep up and stumbles as the dancer behind her continues to advance in well-timed steps. She then runs out of the line, points to her head and indicates that the dancers are crazy, to justify her not being able to keep up with the others. She joins the end of the line and complains to the man in front of her.

While the dancers leave through downstage right, Sagon runs to upstage left to be the first in the coming line. They come in doing the same previous sequence, and Sagon is again pushed out of the line. She begins to speak loudly to the dancers, runs beside them, and insistently tries to get a space in-between them. On her third attempt, she gets back in line, but again only complains, stumbles, and moves her arms and hands in quick and tense gestures while the other dancers move them elegantly. She gets out of the line while the dancers leave the stage. Alone at downstage, she continues talking and complaining.

Sagon runs through the empty stage passing Minarik taking notes, and she calls after the dancers at the door. The music starts. The dancers enter and this time hold their dresses and suits up while running in big steps with knees slightly bent, releasing their weight down at each step. Sagon desperately runs in front of the group as if afraid of being run over. She moves the same body parts as the others, but again with quite different qualities. Sagon's running is tense in quick, small steps, while the group's running is relaxed and fluid. This interaction is repeated several times as the dancers leave the stage and return. Then, at one point, she begins to dismantle the line of dancers by pulling the men out of it. This leads to the beginning of another scene.

In the beginning of the scene, repetition is associated to the "correct attitude" of the group and is the central focus, while difference is associated to the failure of the individual. The evaluating presence of the "ballet *maître*" adds credibility to the pressure for correct learning process. Sagon's partial contrast to the group—keeping the same body parts and locomotion—is an attempt at conforming to it, but exposes her "failure." As Sagon insistently repeats her actions, they become the central focus of the scene, dismantling the notion of "correct" and "incorrect." Sagon's repetitions empower her movement, so that finally she no longer needs to imitate the "right" combination and can even dismantle it.

Repetition as a compositional tool in *1980—A Piece by Pina Bausch* (*1980—Ein Stück von Pina Bausch*) further explores this search for perfection within competitive settings. In an international talent/beauty pageant scene in this piece, the judge speaks the same phrase to some of the contestants in a line downstage (figure 5). The phrase is a limerick that many of the non-native speakers have difficulty repeating, leading to strange nonsensical variations. The audience is presented with the judge's original phrase intermitted with each of the contestants' variations of the phrase spoken in different intonation and timing. The alternation between the original and the failures is rhythmical, constantly juxtaposing the different interpretations with the original. As in the unsuccessful ballet attempts of Dominique Mercy in *Bandoneon*, the focus here is the efforts toward an ideal. The scene criticizes the common notion of perfect repetition without personal input as the ideal. In the scene, failure is what makes the performance interesting. Through repetition, Bausch connects perfect/"correct" with failure/"wrong," inverting the audience's preconceived assumptions. The coexistence of uniformity and variation creates a challenging and aesthetically interesting universe.

The theme of verbal competition continues in a later scene of the same piece. Here, dancers compete to speak at the microphone about their surgeries, scars, and injuries. Finola Cronin says: "I have a broken toe from dashing into a heater; I have a scar on the foot from being run over by a bicycle; I have a scar on the head where a parachute fell on me; I have my spine sutured from falling from a tree; I have a scar on my lip from a dog's bite; I have a scar on the gum where a dentist took out a nerve." Beatrice Libonati points to various parts of her body and says: "Tonsil surgery, appendix surgery, a fall from a chair, cat's scratches, from some performances, here, here, here...and dental surgery." Far from bringing perfection, dance, similar to daily life, produces scars and injuries to the body. It exposes the dancer's body as being similar to everyone else's, disproving the illusion that it is perfect or unattainable.

The dancers around the microphone are suddenly interrupted by the judge (Lutz Förster). He screams to the contestants from the back of the auditorium, asking each one of them by name "What are you afraid of?" Each dancer is forced to reply at increasing volume as the group

Figure 5. The Wuppertal Dance Theater in *1980—A Piece by Pina Bausch*
© Photo by Gert Weigelt www.gert-weigelt.de

gradually retreats upstage. Finola Cronin replies: "Of deep water, of darkness, of everything that jumps. Oh! Frogs." Francis Viet replies: "To become old, that my teeth will fall out, of losing my legs, of going blind, and of being permanently persecuted by someone, of being mutilated." Mechthild Grossmann replies: "Stupidity! Of death. That's enough!" While the judge initially stated an ideal to be achieved by the dancers— the limerick—he now posits a question that reveals their weaknesses. This again exposes the less than ideal makeup of the dancers.

In yet another variation of the competition theme, three women stand side by side while the judge ironically presents each one of them to the audience: "Participant number one recently lost her husband when an airplane crashed into her house. She lost two sons in a car accident. She has debts of more than one thousand marcs and beside that also suffers from grave forms of rheumatism and insomnia. Applause for her! Participant number two was already regularly beaten in childhood. She comes here today from a hospital where her body was in part artificially reconstructed. Her husband is blind and she also suffers from asthma. Applause for her! Participant number three comes here today without family, without friends, without house, without money, and with cancer. Applause for her!"

The participants receive flowers and trophies for their suffering. A wreath is presented to the winner who is identified by the loudest applause for the most suffering endured. The repetition of the competitive settings gradually seem to reward the "wrong" or "abnormal," inverting the notion of conventional competition. It also alludes to society's sado-masochistic common agreement, which validates individual effort expressed through suffering and martyrdom.

The topic of physical pain as related to dance discipline and training is clearly addressed in *Bandoneon*. In the piece, Silvia Kesselheim insistently chases another dancer, trying to wound her legs with scissors. In the process, the victim tells the audience how her ballet teacher used to threaten beginners with scissors if they did not turn out their legs well enough. The painful repetitive "stretching of muscles is demonstrated by dancers forcing the legs of others apart by standing on them with all their weight as they sit cross-legged on the floor....In the large, unfriendly room, the training exercises and dance rituals are isolated into absurd and painful acts of self-dressage" (Servos and Weigelt 1984, 172). This exposes the reality underneath the ethereality of classical ballet dancers in performances.

Repetition—the core of disciplinary learning—is used by Bausch to expose its controlling nature and the painful bodily repression. Foucault's meticulous description of the disciplines developed during the seventeenth and eighteenth centuries may appropriately be applied to the origins of ballet (also developed in the same period):

> The historical moment of the disciplines was the moment when an art of the human body was born, which was directed not only at the growth of its skills, nor at the intensification of its subjection, but at the formation of a relation that in the mechanism itself makes it more obedient as it becomes more useful, and conversely. What was then being formed was a policy of coercions that act upon the body, a calculated manipulation of its elements, its gestures, its behavior. The human body was entering a machinery of power that explores it, breaks it down and rearranges it. A "political anatomy," which was also a "mechanics of power," was being born; it defined how one may have a hold over others' bodies, not only so that they may do what one wishes, but so that they may operate as one wishes, with the techniques, the speed and the efficiency that one determines. Thus discipline produces subjected and practiced bodies, "docile" bodies. Discipline increases the forces of the body (in economic terms of utility) and diminishes these same forces (in political terms of obedience). In short, it dissociates power from the body. (Foucault 1995, 137–138)

Applied to the theatrical setting, Foucault's description exposes dance as a power relationship between the performers and the audience: bodies that should ceaselessly exhibit their abilities to those who pay for it.

Dancers and Audience

Repetition in Bausch's works reveals the body's physical pain and commercial value in theatrical and social power relationships. In a scene of *Arien* (1979), eleven female dancers sit on chairs along the edge of the stage with their eyes closed. Jan Minarik stands behind them and reads out a list of their marketable qualities. Educational, physical, and materialistic assets are given equal value: "Piano, violin, college degree, ballet classes, typewriting, English, French, Spanish, strong thighs, perfect digestive system, German, clean, diligent, intelligent—but not too much (implying a less threatening product, and also a possible reference to the stereotype of dancers as masters of the body and not the mind)—strong, thick muscles, breasts, degree, one Chevrolet, three bedroom apartment, strong teeth." He then continues his sales pitch on the next dancer.

Gradually, a group of male dancers come onstage and start adorning the passive women like dolls. To the light-hearted sounds of Mozart, the women are violated by the men who attempt to make them up as if for a fancy party or wedding ceremony, by combing their hair, inserting balloons as artificial breasts inside their dresses, rudely applying lipstick, and so on (figure 6). Jan Minarik comes to each woman with the microphone and asks: "Can you say 'Ha!'?" The women, now garishly adorned, start pathetically saying "Ha!" continuously. The repetition of this sound, which resembles laughter, is contrasted by the women's inexpressive faces. They obviously don't feel what they express.

Suddenly, the increasing interjections are overlapped by the discourse of one of the dancers. Silvia Kesselheim stands up from her chair and reads a newspaper report into the microphone. She describes a Danish contortionist performing in England who was carried to the hospital screaming in pain from his dislocated hips, with his head and legs locked into a knot; he performed again the next day even though the doctor had prohibited him to do so. Kesselheim then reads another report about painful beauty enhancing daily actions and surgical procedures. She then reads a report on a beauty pageant held in Wiesbaden. At this point, the increasingly loud pathetic laughter by the rest of the group drowns out Kesselheim's reading. Gradually louder "Ha!" sounds strengthen the group breathing and posture, evoking anger instead of fun.

In this critical picture of social coercion, the men force/deform the women's bodies to "beautify" them in order to please their buyers—the audience. Bausch's works are not the display of socially agreed "beautiful" movements. Instead, they are a critique of the social concept of beauty, and of the individual's sacrifice within theatrical and social relationships to achieve such an ideal. Gradually, a perverted concept of the women's beauty emerges from the constructed make-up and clothing. In fact, the scene is beautiful—visually and musically impressive in its movement composition and theatrical effects. While witnessing the distortion of preconceived notions of beauty, the audience listens to narrative of physical and painful distortions. Later in the same piece,

Figure 6. Josephine Ann Endicott and Christian Trouillas in *Arien*
© Photo by Gert Weigelt www.gert-weigelt.de

Jakob Andersen tries several times to bring his legs over his head, connecting the contortionist's efforts to the compulsive nature of dance.

The make-up scene in *Arien* dismantles dance as the spontaneous expression of inner states, as well as the conventions usually associated with the everyday act of laughing. In the beginning, such an act is associated with being violated and lacking emotion. This gives way to laughter becoming an expression of anger. Repetition establishes a signifying chain in which meaning is constantly challenged and transformed. Then, laughter becomes screams, expressive of desperation under the all-controlling power of social coercion. As in Benati's screams, desperation and change emerge from the chain of mechanical, repetitive actions. The transitory meaning comes from the repetitive form and is itself about the form. Spontaneity is an unexpected experience that happens only through such changeable linguistic structure.

The act of laughter is a common audience reaction in this and in many of Bausch's scenes (Bentivoglio 1994, 18). As the male dancers over-adorned and deformed the passive women, the audience laughed at their absurd appearance. Gradually, such expected reaction was incorporated and distorted in the scene, leaving the audience perplexed. As interpreted by Norbert Servos and Gert Weigelt, "[t]he explorations of dance theater are equivalent to repeated checks on the forms of behavior acquired and accepted without thought....With a nudge and a wink, the onlooker is made an accomplice to the unmasking; laughing together makes it easy to shrug off the compulsions" (1984, 24).

By repeating and changing the audience's reaction—laughter—the scene establishes a constant dialogue between dancers and audience. Through such means, Bausch revives a differentiated sense of responsibility and awareness:

> Tragedy presupposes guilt, despair, moderation, lucidity, vision, a sense of responsibility. In the Punch-and-Judy show of our century, in this backsliding of the white race, there are neither guilty nor responsible individuals anymore. No one could do anything about it, and no one wanted to. Indeed, things happen without anyone in particular being responsible for them. Everything is dragged along and everyone gets caught somewhere in the sweep of events. We are all collectively guilty, collectively bogged down in the sins of our fathers and of our forefathers. We are the children of our forebears. That is our misfortune, but not our guilt....Comedy is the only thing that can still reach us...the tragic is still possible even if pure tragedy is not. We can achieve the

tragic out of comedy, we can bring it forth as a frightening moment, as an abyss
that opens suddenly. (Dürrenmatt 1982, 254–255)

At first, the grotesque appearances exposed the tragic-comic, gradually
transformed into comic-tragic. Suddenly, the audience watches its own
uncompromising laughter being publicly exposed as anger and
desperation.

Three themes from *Arien* can also be seen in *1980*: the distortion of
laughter; the equal valuation of the human body and material goods; the
relationship between active and passive participants. In the second act of
1980, Lutz Förster comes onstage and declares his love and respect to an
empty chair in front of him: "My beloved chair, for many times you are
used without attention, and I have to tell you once and for all how you
are dear to me and how much I admire you. You are not only elegant and
practical, but you were also ingeniously constructed. You have four legs,
which sit on the ground as a cliff in the breaking of the waves. But you
are not minimally comparable to any little bench. No. You also have a
back. But you know very well that you don't have arms, because you
don't want to facilitate too much the life of those who use you. They
would have to act with awareness and think where they rest their arms.
Your color is of timeless elegance. You are simply beautiful. I am proud
of you. Recently I sat on you. Of course, you don't remember it
anymore. This is not any criticism! I understand…with all the mess that
has happened around here! No, I am not jealous. But to tell you the truth,
I would like you to exist only for me. And I wish from the bottom of my
heart that you are not busy next time I need you. And if you feel any
empathy toward my feelings, give me a little sign."

The audience laughs effusively in the face of such absurd behavior.
He then puts the chair on a little platform on the center of the stage and
repeats the same love declaration, interrupting it with forced and
increasingly louder laughter. He has now become simultaneously the
dancer and the audience. As the women in *Arien*, the dancer—chair—on
the platform here is both strong and passively silent. Dance is not the
actions of the female dancers or chair, but the audience's interactions
with what is onstage.

This distorted effect of repetition can also be found in *Kontakthof*
and in *Bandoneon*, where the audience's applause is included in the stage
performance. As described in chapter 3, in *Kontakthof*, performers

portray the audience's applause, as a reward for the dancers' acts of bodily torture.

In one sequence of *Bandoneon*, all the female dancers applaud each individual male dancer. In return, the males applaud each female, until every dancer has been applauded at least three times. In this dance about the narcissism of the art itself, the dancers are both the performers and the admirers. However, those who applaud and represent the audience are much more active than those who receive the applause and are simply posing onstage. It seems like the group of dancers applauds for the sake of it, without discretion. Dance becomes the need to applaud.

Through repetition, applause is changed from being a sign of recognition of actions onstage. Instead, it conveys the inexhaustible need for the audience to give and the dancers to receive a reward. Performance itself onstage is not fulfilling for either dancers or audience members. Repetition reveals the theatrical split between "doers" and "watchers" as necessarily alienating and unsatisfactory.

After each dancer is applauded several times, Jan Minarik flexes his arm like a body-builder posing in front of the group to the point of exhaustion. Despite his extensive effort to please his stage audience, he receives only weak applause from them. Individual effort and sacrifice does not automatically bring social recognition. It is the audience that determines the *value* of the performance by applauding or withholding it.

The theme of dance as a sale of performing bodies is also explored in a scene of *Kontakthof*, commenting on the separation of sexual roles within this aesthetic-commercial environment. The piece starts with the stage dimly lit, with all the dancers sitting on chairs along the three stage walls. Josephine Ann Endicott stands up, comes downstage, and performs a sequence of movements as if showing off her body for sale to the audience. She first stands upright facing forward, turns backward and slowly glides her hands over her hair through the back of her neck, turns forward and smiles as if just to show her teeth, then turns sideways and tucks her pelvis forward and up and back in place, and finally returns to her chair. Before she is even finished, two other female dancers are already doing the same sequence by her side. Then one man starts, suddenly followed by all the men, and next by all the women, doing the same sequence. Women and men meet briefly downstage, at which point the women are facing backward and the man, forward, in an alternating line that is visually catching.

In the beginning, when Endicott does her movements, the audience laughs a great deal. There is a remarkable contrast between her cynical performance and the stillness of the rest of the group sitting along the stage walls. Gradually, as the whole group repeats Endicott's sequence and dismantles its uniqueness, the audience becomes silent as it watches dancers becoming both dealers and objects of the stage sale. Dance's traditional separation of roles is not erased as in abstract dances in which all dancers dress alike and perform abstract shapes. Sexual differentiation is highlighted in this organized body market. Gender and capitalism in dance are critically addressed as the piece's main subject. Dancers not only perform movements for sale. They dance the sale of movements.

Women and Men

The relationship between the sexes is explored throughout *Kontakthof.* Similar to the relationship between dancers and audience described earlier, repetition exposes separation, dissatisfaction, and dependency between the male and female dancers. The attempts of union with a partner, even if starting with tender gestures, soon evolves into reciprocal aggression and frustration.

In one scene, while the dancers sit on chairs along the stage walls, Meryl Tankard walks downstage with her eyes closed guided by Dominique Mercy. He returns to his seat, while Tankard with her eyes closed proceeds to perform tender and intimate movements, as if trying to feel her body. She glides her right hand delicately over her left arm, carefully smells her right arm, slightly rubs her right ankle over the left one twice. She softly touches parts of her face, glides both hands along her hair, slowly arranges the underwear at her waist, and then restarts the movements. In the middle of her second performance, Arthur Rosenfeld comes downstage and accompanies her back to her chair along the wall.

Another male dancer brings Josephine Ann Endicott downstage. Also with her eyes closed, she performs another self-caressing sequence. She slightly presses two fingers of her right hand to her navel, quickly touches different areas of her breasts and stomach, as if checking if they were still there. She then lightly and slowly glides her right hand along her chest toward her face, and brings her head downward with both arms crossed over her chest. She pauses embracing herself, then drops the right strap of her dress and kisses her bare right shoulder. She puts the strap back in place and restarts. Again, another male dancer comes to take her back to her chair.

Anne Martin is also brought downstage by yet another male dancer. With her eyes closed, she performs light and slow movements. She feels her face with her right hand, stretches her right arm high, lets it fall over the top of her head and begins caressing it. She bends her long, slim body forward and touches the arch of her right foot with her right hand, and slowly scratches it two or three times. She then smells the upper inside part of her left arm, touches her lips with one of her fingers, and delicately touches her buttocks with both hands.

The audience laughs at Martin's relaxed and deliberate foot scratching. In everyday life, such an action is often done with a sense of urgency to relieve uncomfortable itching. Martin does not seem to want to quickly eliminate the itching. In these self-caressing rituals performed by women, repetition is dissociated from mechanization, evoking an "inexhaustible need for love," present in even a simple routine act such as scratching (Bentivoglio 1990, 20). Soon all the other female dancers begin to perform personal sequences of self-caressing.

Gradually, the men come downstage and perform their sequences. Differing from the women, all the men perform simultaneously, paired up with women, men, or alone. Alongside Meryl Tankard doing her sequence, Jean-Laurent Sasportes performs his. He touches his lips with his right hand, and pauses for a moment. He lightly taps his right thigh, touches his buttocks, slightly raising up on his toes, glides his left hand over his hair and the back of his neck, and then restarts.

Gradually, the need for caressing becomes an impulse toward interaction, and some of the dancers begin to perform their sequences on their partners. Nonetheless, rather than satisfactory, such interaction is shown to be invasive, interruptive, and aggressive. Sasportes starts tapping Tankard's thigh, and touching her lips and buttocks instead of his own, while she continues to perform her sequence. He embraces her from behind, slightly lifting her off the ground. They turn toward each other, and she also starts doing her sequence on him. She gently touches the interior side of his right arm; he taps her left thigh while she glides her hands along his hair; he embraces her and lightly lifts her off the ground.

The duet becomes increasingly aggressive. Instead of gliding his left hand over Tankard's hair, he grabs it and pulls her head back in a sudden and sharp impulse. She resists as he forces his fingers over her lips and tries to tap her thighs. He taps her buttocks and bounces her up and down from behind. As their movements become quicker, tenser, and stronger, they look like a couple fighting. He forces his hand over her face and taps on her right thigh; she touches his face almost in a slap and twists his nose; he vigorously lifts her up and down a couple of times, while she hangs loose and straight in his arms as her face increasingly begins to show discomfort. He turns over her to tap her left thigh, but she bends over to protect herself, before running off stage. In a compulsive search for caressing, one not only touches oneself but also reaches out to others. But this only establishes a physically imposed power relationship between the sexes.

Later in the same piece, the dancers are separated in two groups by gender. The groups start confronting each other through words that provoke body movement. Arthur Rosenfeld, speaking for the men's group, says: "Hand, cheek, back, stomach, knee." The women's group retreats, with each member contracting her body as if being punched in the mentioned body parts. Then Josephine Ann Endicott, on behalf of the women's group, speaks out the same body parts, and the men respond with associated body movements. The reciprocal verbal attacks followed by corporal responses continue with increased intensity as the two groups approach each other. In this dispute for power between the sexes, verbal language affects and determines body gesture. Interestingly, when the power struggle was physical, the males dominated, but when it is verbal, the playing field becomes even.

At one point, when both groups are quite close to each other, the intensity diminishes. Endicott speaks in a soft, low voice to the men: "Hand, cheek." Rosenfeld does the same to the women's group. Then they gradually make a transition back to the self-caressing scene. This time, instead of performing solos as the women, or in pairs as the men, they perform it in groups divided by gender. Each group starts repeating in unison a sequence originally done by one of its own members. Although the groups perform a different sequence from each other, some similarities exist within these movements which are sometimes performed simultaneously by both groups—for example, foot scratching.

This creates a composition of order and chance, differences and similarities.

The groups gradually approach and merge with each other while continuing to repeat their sequences. They form male-female couples and do their own group's sequence on their partners' bodies. As the woman touches the man's nose, he glides his hands along her hair and head; she feels his buttocks, while he touches her face; as she touches his face, he touches her right wrist; she lets her right hand fall over his head and caresses his hair, while he rubs her upper arm; she scratches his foot, he scratches her navel area. Although performing the same reciprocal movements, each couple has a different timing. The scene becomes an intricate net of relationships expressed through the alternation and simultaneity of repetitive movement sequences.

As in the previous mutual caressing scene, this too develops into physical aggression. Their movements become more intense, until they all end up pulling each other's hair, slapping each other's faces, etc. The scene begins to look like a chaotic fight, where the men try to strike the women while they try to defend themselves.

Through repetition, verbally manifested aggression moves toward tenderness and reverts to physical aggression. Neither aggression nor tenderness satiates the individual needs within social relationships. The scene challenges the convention of dancers as connected to and fulfilled by their physicality. It also contradicts the convention of dance as physical presence onstage, for these bodies are actually marked by absence and the insatiable need for the other.

Bodies and Words

In *Arien*, repetition verbally dominates the body and exposes it as an unsatisfied object. In the piece, eight dancers individually describe an unique part of their bodies in a repetitive and playful structure. They do this while slowly walking toward the audience and gazing at it. In the beginning, the first dancer describes his/her unique body part, and each of the others repeats the description while substituting their own unique body part. In the next set, the second dancer describes his/her body part, and the others repeat it while inserting their own body part. Though the original description is logically meaningful, the next ones evoke grotesque or surreal images, making a parallel between normality and deformation. This social body, described through borrowed phrases, is shown to be not perfect, complete, or unique.

Following are the initial descriptions: "My shoulder is bony." "My eye is bony." "My nose is bony " "My foot is bony." "My tooth is bony." "My kneecap is bony." "My stomach is bony." "My belly button is bony." "My nose has two holes." "My foot has two holes." "My tooth has two holes." "My kneecap has two holes." "My stomach has two holes." "My belly button has two holes." "My shoulder has two holes." "My eye has two holes." "I have two kneecaps." "I have two stomachs." "I have two belly buttons." "I have two shoulders." "I have two eyes." "I have two noses." "I have two feet." "I have two teeth." Following this, two dancers leave the scene.

Within this plot, meaning is constantly distorted and rearranged, establishing a repetitive net between the different phrases. The game contrasts words for body parts and the semantic structures about and around them. Body pieces are constantly exchanged and distorted, becoming the reinforced subject. If, as addressed in chapter 3, repetition initially places dance as Symbolic language and not as "motor manifestations" (Lacan 1988, 255), it now gradually evokes the physicality of dance within a game of signifiers.

And the game continues: "My bad tooth is loose." "My bad kneecap is loose." "My stomach is loose." "My eye is loose." "My nose is loose." "My foot is loose." The term "loose" is part of the everyday lexicon of some dance techniques, as dancers loosen up for performances. Here, dancers loosen not only conventional body parts such as neck, back, and shoulders, but also their stomach, eyes, nose, and teeth. They take the dancers' preparation to absurdity, expanding dance's borders. This also shows the dancers' narcissistic preoccupation with their bodies.

Approaching the audience, the game continues with only four dancers who complain: "I can't see my stomach." "I can't see my nose." "I can't see my foot." "I can't see my kneecap." They then ask the audience: "Have you seen my kneecap?" "Have you seen my stomach?" "Have you seen my nose?" "Have you seen my foot?"

In dance, the artist's body is the central art object. This has led to the misconception that dance is the only art form to imply a sense of wholeness between artwork and artist. This convention presupposes the dance work as complete in itself, independent from its (passive) audience. As already described, this is not the case in Bausch's works, where the spectators' reactions—applause, laughter, curious gaze—are critically included in the dance. The sentences from *Arien* described above evoke the absence of the dancers' body parts and their inability to see their own artwork from the spectators' point of view. Instead of implying wholeness, dance's congruency between artist and artwork is fragmentary.

Theatrical dance requires a "doer"/insider and a "viewer"/outsider of the performed movement. Already in their training, dancers become used to seeing themselves through their inverted and two-dimensional reflection on the mirror—as an outside observer. While trying to feel their bodies, dancers are guided by an artificial external image, developing a fragmented perception.

For Jacques Lacan, "the mirror serves as a metaphor and a structural concept at the same time that it points to a crucial experience in [the] psychic development" of the narcissistic ego (Ragland-Sullivan 1986, 29). As in dance, the mirror in Lacan's developmental theory represents the child's illusion of wholeness with an outer image. This phase evolves into the child's recognition of its split between self and Other—"the social order of language, myths and conventions" (Lacan in Ragland-Sullivan 1986, 16). The mirror stage is the birth of the fragmented body-image, triggering the child's incorporation—repetition—of its external/social-familial body images, in search for unity. The child can only recognize, and identify itself as a body when confronted with a non-identical external image:

> Our identity evolves in a paradoxical context, then, out of a feeling of Oneness, which is really made up of two beings (*le trait unaire*). Nevertheless, ...this "little reality" (*ce peu de réalité*), the spatial captivation or fixation by the mother's *imago*, determine humans as already alienated from other beings in all later endeavors. (Ragland-Sullivan 1986, 29)

The sentences spoken by the dancers dismantle the mirror stage illusion of completion with the other. This suggests their identity as marked by fragmentation and dependency.

In Bausch's works, the mechanism of the mirror is used to invert and question the roles of dancers and spectators. The dancers not only incorporate the viewers' perspective by critically performing applause and laughter, but they also incite the viewers to incorporate the dancers' perspective. In this scene's sentences, the dancers ask the audience about body parts usually seen by the viewers, such as foot and nose, as well as body parts unseen by the viewer but sensed by the mover, such as kneecap and stomach.

The sentences remind the audience that there is much one cannot see in any apparent movement. There is no single way a movement should be seen and interpreted. Dance is seen and unseen movement conceived through words. Even as the dancers ask the audience about their body parts that they seem unable to locate, the dancers' bodies become more visible approaching downstage. Dance becomes a contradictory dialogue between dancers and audience, between words and movements, and it is constantly searching for its own language.

The game continues with the dancers declaring their love for their own body parts, suggesting more deformations: "I love my nose." "I love my foot." "I love my kneecap." "I love my stomach." "My stomach is under my heart." "My nose is under my heart." "My foot is under my heart." "My kneecap is under my heart."

The sentences continue to displace body parts, but now in relation to a daily body movement: "I walk on my foot." "I walk on my kneecap." "I walk on my stomach." "I walk on my nose." The sentences imply that different body parts—seen and unseen—are not only part of, but are also the support for, a basic locomotive pattern. Verbal statements expand the movement possibilities of the body, from a simple walking on the feet to the most bizarre and physically impossible action, such as walking on the nose. The dancers upset any expectations the audience may have for technical movements and the display of physical abilities; instead, they only walk and talk onstage like everyday people. This variation is a critique to the stereotype of dancers as bodies capable of performing the most amazing movements with perfection.

The dancer's statements also unsettle body alignment, which is a fundamental dance concept. Instead of balancing body parts within their "adequate" places, the statements fragment the body and reorganize it in a distorted form. This is a break from the primordial notion of a coherent and unified psychophysical identity.

According to Lacan, during the first months of life, a child does not experience a bodily or psychic unity: "Its body is an aggregate of uncoordinated parts, zones, sensations, necessities and impulses, instead of an integrated totality" (Lacan in Grosz 1990, 28). It only becomes a unity as it merges with its environment and mother. In a subsequent moment, the child is able to perceive itself as a distinct body by recognizing the absence of the (m)other. Its identity is then based on the split between inner and outer and the necessary absence of the outer. This psychological split corresponds to the semiotic split between signified and signifier.

Through body and verbal language, the child will try to unite itself again with the desired outer image. It gradually incorporates these outer images, building up a Symbolic/social body. This socially formed identity gives the individual apparent security and support, but it is based on lack and dependency. Lacan describes it as an "orthopaedic" form of totality (1977, 4).

If the "machinery of power" (Foucault 1995, 137) disjoints and recomposes the body for its domination, Bausch's dance theater re-makes these processes in order to re-associate power to the body. The scene in *Arien* evokes a fragmented body-image with neither the early comfort of completeness with the mother, nor the later support of a socially structuring image. The verbal statements bring about the trauma of the fragmented body (Hillman and Mazzio 1997) that has been forgotten in the unconscious:

> This fragmented body...usually manifests itself in dreams when the movement of the analysis encounters a certain level of aggressive disintegration in the individual. It then appears in the form of disjointed limbs, or of those organs represented in exoscopy, growing wings and taking up arms for intestinal persecutions...this form is even tangibly revealed at the organic level, in the lines of "fragilization" that define the anatomy of phantasy, as exhibited in the schizoid and spasmodic symptoms of hysteria. (Lacan 1977, 4–5)

Such pathological "fragilization" of the body can be illustrated by the dancers' next sentences: "My nose is irritated." "My foot is irritated." "My kneecap is irritated." "My stomach is irritated." The incorporation of external images by this fragmented body is not an abstract process, but one that is physically intrusive: "I've got another kneecap." "I've got another stomach." As in the dancers' description of their scars and surgeries in *1980*'s competition scene, verbal language in this example evokes the dancers' imperfect and damaged bodies. Injuries and surgeries are part of dancers' lives. During the 1994 season of the Company in Wuppertal, Regina Advento (figure 7) was not performing

Figure 7. Pina Bausch and Regina Advento
© Photo by Euler Paixão

due to impending knee surgery. Upon further inquiry, she revealed that her dance training started at the age of four, and that now her right leg stretches to such an extent that her kneecap pops out of place.

Then the last three dancers left onstage declare ownership and emotional ties to body parts they acquired from others: "My nose is beautiful." "My foot is beautiful." "I like my stomach." "I like my nose." In *Arien*'s verbal chains, the body echoes as the final victim of a social coercive process. Through repetition, the dancers expose and insist on the recognition of a physical pain and desire beyond words.

In *Kontakthof*, painful repetitive masochistic acts (chapter 3) were posited as artificially produced solely to receive audience (stage) applause, dismantling pain as an authentic experience. Yet, in the scene of *Arien*, the *description* of pain as a *method* is dismantled. According to Elaine Scarry, pain's essential nature resists its accurate description through language; pain is unsharable, unshowable, and unseeable.

> [Nonetheless,] there come to be avenues by which this most radically private of experiences begins to enter the realm of public discourse....Perhaps the most obvious is medicine, for the success of the physician's work will often depend on the acuity with which he or she can hear the fragmentary language of pain, coax it into clarity, and interpret it. (1985, 4–6)

Therefore, *Arien*'s repetitive scene incorporates and distorts the method of empirical medical discourse.

According to Foucault (1994), modern positivist medicine began at the end of the eighteenth century, also the period of ballet's development. The birth of modern medicine was marked by the development of a rational discourse believed to represent the truth about the body's diseases, identifying them through the doctor's all-seeing gaze, locating the diseases, "spatializing" them in the "anatomical atlas" of the patient's body, and controlling them (3). Diseases and their controlling procedures were organized according to the patient's similar (repetitious) and serial complaints: "The individual in question was not so much a sick person as the endlessly reproducible pathological fact to be found in all patients suffering in a similar way" (97). Exhaustive description through such rational discourse became the clinic's main means. Different diseases were seen not as unsettling and new, but only as a set of new combinations of the old ones, and therefore equally controllable through their systematization and description. Diseases became expected repetitions (97).

Criticizing the clinic, Foucault affirms that medicine's attempt to organize and control diseases multiplies them beyond simple combinations. This is shown in *Arien*'s scene, which multiplies a disease through repetitive discourse. The first phrase is passed to the next person as in an epidemic chain, which not only proliferates the disease, but also mutates its symptoms. According to Foucault, an epidemic is an individual and social happening not based on the isolated individual and its specialized observation and treatment. It is a web that weaves from one person to the other, within a specific time and place. "Being a collective phenomenon, it requires a multiple gaze; a unique process, it must be described in terms of its special, accidental, unexpected qualities" (25). Thus, it is simultaneously repetitive and unpredictable. Similarly, Bausch's works are intrinsically contradictory: marked by repetition within collective events, and at the same time challenging predictions, *a priori* and one-sided perspectives.

Foucault further states that the clinical discourse is based on the assumption of the all seeing/knowing clinical eye. Exhaustive description of the symptom/signifier would decipher and control the disease/signified. However, in *Arien*, repetitive descriptions are used to contradict rational understanding, dismantling the power imposed on the body through an *a priori* knowledge. Exhaustible and repetitive descriptions increasingly confound and distance the audience from any final truth.

Descriptions contradict visual experience. As they approach the audience and become more visible, the dancers refer to the disappearance and invisibility of their bodies ("I can't see my stomach....Have you seen my stomach?" "I can't see my nose....Have you seen my nose?"). Unlike clinical descriptions, these are unable to provide insight into both internal and external body parts. What is visible parallels what is not, dissociating visibility from reality.

Just like the doctor controlling gazes at the patient to gather information, the audience gazes at the dancers in a one-way power relationship. However, in *Arien*—and in many of Bausch's works—the dancers gaze back at the audience. By repeating the audience's action, the dancers include themselves in the empowering position of the observer, dismantling the traditional one-way relationship. Like the mirroring water covering the stage floor, dancers reflect back the audience's gaze. As described by Arlene Raven:

> Lines between water and shore, stage and seats, can be drawn and shifted with metaphoric ease. Such an exchange of the boundaries of substantive form is signaled by the rise of the house lights. I think *Arien* has ended and stand. It is just then that I notice performers looking curiously at me; a few people laugh nervously and one dancer has joined us in the balcony. We, an audience observed, cross the line into the water. (1985, 75)

As a positivist science, modern medicine was born out of a negative aspect—the lack of health—and it works in a positive aspect—the presence of care and cure. Its mechanism establishes an opposition between health and morbidity, normal and pathological. Its aim is to erase sickness and provide mastered, healthy, and productive bodies. Also in a positivist approach, ballet developed as a system of repetitions to master the human body. Its major aim is the erasure of movement failure and the establishment of technically and expressively perfect bodies.

The repetitive method of medicine and ballet bring scars, failure, injuries, and weaknesses in Bausch's works. The choreographer uses the positivist method to invert the conventional dichotomies of perfect-imperfect, healthy-sick, and normal-abnormal. Repetition posits supposedly perfect ballet dancers as injured or imperfect, associating this condition with normality. As in the interminable rituals of caressing and aggression in *Kontakthof*, repetition exposes a constant neediness and unfulfillment, instead of positivism's completeness and satisfaction. The essentially negative basis of medicine and ballet—structured around the *absence* of health and movement perfection, respectively—becomes dance's ultimate means and subject. Through the controlling method present in science and art, the Wuppertal Dance Theater criticizes and dismantles the positivist structure of knowledge and power over the body—the group of pre(de)formed ideas that "for two hundred years...have constituted the dark, but firm web of our experience" (Foucault 1994, 199).

5
THROUGH REPETITION:
THE ABSENCE OF MEANING
AND THE MEANING OF ABSENCE

One day, hidden from herself, she marked down in her expense book some sentences about the Sugar Loaf. Only a few words, she was laconic. A long time after that, in one lonely afternoon, she remembered she had written something about something—the Sugar Loaf? The sea? She looked for the expenses book. All over the house. Object by Object....What a disaster—she said—motionless in the middle of the living room, without direction, without knowing where to look....Don't get downhearted, she said to herself, look for it among the papers, among the letters, among the rare news people used to send. Ah, had they written her more she would have many papers and would have more places to look. But her ordered life was exposed, had few hiding places, it was clean. In her house the only hiding place was herself. But what a happiness to have furniture, boxes in which to find things by chance. She had enough places to look indefinitely.

    Clarice Lispector (1992)

Dances were not created out of joy, but out of a need. To withstand these needs, to follow up on their reasons, was from the beginning an important focus for the poetic excursions of the Wuppertaler Tanztheater.

    Pina Bausch and Norbert Servos (quoted in Erler, 1994)

Dance as Incompleteness and Desire

In Lacan's narcissistic ego theory, the child's recognition of the mother's absence marks the split between self and other, internal and external, subject and object: "From this time on, lack, gap, splitting will be its mode of being" (Grosz 1990, 35). Within the Symbolic order, the search for completeness and meaning through verbal and gestural language does not bring communication and repose. The signifying chain constantly multiplies and challenges meanings, further increasing the desire and need. Thus, identities are constructed on this constant search for outer completeness and recurring loss through and within language.

Repetition in Bausch's choreography upsets the illusion of the dancers and the audience of outside completion. Dancers repeat their movement and words as if they had not made themselves clear the first time. The audience watches these re-presentations, which instead of clarifying their meaning, dismantle them and recreate others. Dance addresses its gap of communication between dancers and audience, instigating more repetitions.

Repetition initially establishes a signifying chain in which dance's meaning is constantly shifting. Eventually, these recurrent disencounters with meaning become repetition's ultimate significance. As addressed by Lacan, underneath the signifying chain are no instincts, only vacuum. Repetition evokes a reflexive meaning about its inherently hollow structure. By conveying its lack of meaning-fulfillment as meaning, repetition at the same time contradicts and reaffirms itself as absence and need. Repetition reaffirms its structural quality of never positing a final and definite meaning, constantly affirming and contradicting itself.

The insatiable search for outer completion within the dancers-audience relationship is the means and subject of two scenes of *On a Mountain a Cry Was Heard* (*Auf dem Gebirge hat man ein Geschrei gehört,* 1984). In the first act, Bénédicte Billiet and another female dancer come onstage dressed as teenagers in the 1950s in high heels and pastel-colored party dresses. They walk side by side downstage, holding hands, smiling, and chatting. They look seductively at the audience in a childlike manner, shrinking their shoulders and feigning shyness.

The two dancers then stand side by side at arms length, facing opposite directions. They secretly glance at the audience and whisper to each other as if preparing to do something surprising. Suddenly, they perform cartwheels back-and-forth from each other. They arrange their dresses back in place and begin behaving in their childish/seductive manner while walking toward downstage left. They continue to perform these series of acts until they are dragged off-stage by Jan Minarik. Even as they leave the stage, the dancers continue to behave seductively toward the audience. The effect of the dancers' simultaneous cartwheels with their dresses up in the air is visually beautiful. The audience laughs and applauds the dancers in an acknowledgment of their theatrical and physical abilities.

As with playing children performing cartwheels to show off their skills, the dancers seem to be acting out to get the audience's attention.

The dance in *Mountain* is not only technically and visually impressive, but it also has a playful, seductive interaction with the audience. Here dance is a reflexive critique on its own narcissistic nature, existing for the other (the viewer).

In *Mountain*, the stage floor is covered with mud. In the second act, male dancers and stagehands gradually bring large trees—trunk and leaves—and place them onstage before letting them fall. This is done in a staggered manner that alternates between the entrance, placement, and falling of the trees—a total of thirty-two are brought onstage. This creates an image of a forest simultaneously being built and destroyed. Accompanied by orchestral music, the visual effect also suggests a dancing composition of trees. This sets the tone for additional spectacular events to follow.

Bénédicte Billiet comes back onstage and performs another series of movements while seductively looking at the audience and occasionally hiding behind the trees. These movements are initially entertaining but soon become repetitive. Then, Beatrice Libonati comes onstage holding a white sheet over her naked body and carrying a second white sheet and pillow under the other arm. At center stage, while holding the first sheet over her body, Libonati arranges the other sheet and the pillow as if fixing a bed, and loudly speaks to the audience: "Hello! Come on! Night!" Nobody appears to her beckoning. She then rearranges herself under the sheet and repeats the offer several times, while Billiet continues her seductive sequence.

At a certain point, Billiet leaves the stage and the music ends. Libonati's words then resonate more acutely through the silent stage. Laying on top of the mud in-between thirty-two fallen trees, a lonely woman insists on rearranging her clean white bed and calling out for her beloved—the audience. Instead of a grand theatrical encore, the audience is presented with an image of profound individual loneliness and need for the other. Male dancers and stage-hands come onstage and casually remove the trees while Libonati continues her call. As the trees are taken away, the audience is confronted with an empty and silent stage reinforced by Libonati's unfulfilled plea for love. Absence, desire, and dissatisfaction echo on the *Mountain*.

As another scene begins ignoring Libonati's presence, she leaves the stage. In this scene, a couple plays a repetitive, courting game. The female dancer "accidentally" drops her scarf. In an elaborate movement, the male dancer jumps and catches the scarf, and gallantly returns it to her. She keeps dropping the scarf, and he keeps retrieving it. Libonati's intimate call for love is substituted by a young couple's cute seductive game. While both scenes are repetitive, Libonati calls out for someone non-existent in the audience, and the female dancer in the couple scene manipulates an existent dancer onstage. The collage of scenes confounds feelings of loneliness and sadness with the pleasure of watching the fun game. By enjoying the new scene, we feel almost as inattentive and negligent to Libonati's need as the men taking away the trees.

Repetition is structural in the four events: The falling of thirty-two trees, Billiet's seductive sequence, Libonati's call for love, and the couple's seductive game. Be it between dancers, or between dancer and audience, relationships are posited here as nets of dependency, dissatisfaction, and recurrence.

Still again in *Mountain*, another scene evokes the dancer's constant need and search through repetitive movements. As described in chapter 3, the second act begins with Libonati—with her hair painted white—who had remained onstage throughout the intermission. She then leaves, and the second scene begins with Lutz Förster and Dominique Mercy, dressed in black suits, elegant black shoes, and white shirts, standing still downstage right. Förster performs rounded movements with his hands and arms, with free flow, light weight, and varied time. The momentum of these movements propels him forward, and he begins running with his arms stretched out in front of him as if reaching out for someone. His running across the stage is interrupted by Mercy who places a chair in his path. Förster touches the chair with his hand, pauses, and looks at the audience. The sequence of rounded arm-movements, running across the stage, and looking at the audience is repeated a number of times, with Mercy interrupting it with the placement of a table, piano, blanket, and napkin.

At upstage, Förster touches Mercy's shoulder and both stand side by side backward to the audience. As a cabaret song begins, they turn and gently look at the audience. They repeatedly turn toward and away from the audience, alternating gaze with no-gaze. Such simple gestures become dance accompanied by music.

Center stage, with their backs to the audience, they perform a few steps in unison to the beat of the cabaret song. They gradually advance toward the audience, maintaining their upper bodies almost immobile.

Dance, initially posited as a continuous and insatiable search, is now the presence of released bodies, doing almost imperceptible movements that bring them closer and closer to the audience. As they approach the audience, looking at it pleadingly, the lyrics of the song in the background state: "Maybe it's because I love you too much. Maybe that's why you love me so little....Maybe if I loved you less; maybe you would love me more....Maybe it's because I kiss you too much....Maybe it's because my kiss means so little....Maybe I'll be left with no love at all." Then at center stage, they stop and look at the audience as if expecting acknowledgment for their "little dance." Like the "little kiss," their dance might mean "so little" since the audience expected more from these accomplished dancers. Nonetheless, they dance "too much" for the audience and may "be left with no love [and attention] at all."

As the song ends, Förster restarts his arm sequence and runs toward a dark corner of the stage. He stops as he touches Mercy's shoulder, and they leave the stage, performing an abbreviated version of the simple steps duet, with Förster intermittently touching Mercy's shoulder. In the meantime, Libonati comes back onstage in a summer dress with her hair wet and clean. She runs across the stage blowing kisses to the audience in a light and playful manner. This contrasts with her character before the Förster/Mercy scene in which she stood crying with her hair painted white. As with the previous collage of scenes—Billiet's hiding, Libonati's call for love, the couple's courting ritual—Bausch here alternates and juxtaposes different emotional states.

Similar to Josephine Ann Endicott running in circles in the same piece (chapter 3), Förster's compulsive running is initiated by rounded shapes of the upper body in free flow, emphasizing an uncontrollable internal impulse searching for a goal. From the beginning of Förster's scene, the highly trained ballet dancers do not perform a series of technical movements. Instead, their movements represent search and void. The audience's expectations are disappointed at each one of Förster's repetitions. When the viewer thinks they will finally start "dancing," they perform a simple sequence as if casually filling up performance time. Dance steps become matter of fact, while Förster's recurrent searches become the dance event. The dancers' search for completion (with the audience) is reinforced by the substitution of their duet by Libonati who throws kisses to the audience members.

Breaking Through the Symbolic:
The Real as Absence

In Bausch's works, the dancers' recurrent attempts toward external completion provoke repeated instances of disappointment and stillness. At moments, the dancers unexpectedly hesitate without much action and pathetically just face the audience. It seems that they do not have any material to re-present to the audience or do not even have any idea as to what to do. By incorporating dance's inherent split and incompleteness, dance theater brings frightening moments of "non-representation" on to the stage. Repetition brings about a break through re-presentation, like "an abyss that opens suddenly" (Dürrenmatt 1982, 255). Paradoxically, the real is encountered through the (repetitive) failures of the Symbolic.

Lacan distinguished two main forces within psychoanalysis: the insistence of the signs—"automaton," repetition—and the encounter with the Real—*tuché* (Lacan 1978, 53–64). The Real always lies behind the automaton, as presence lies behind fantasy. The Real is manifested by its absence, by the trauma of the missed encounter (the split between self and other). Instead of bringing completion, the encounters with reality are marked by "abeyance" and pain:

> It is this that we have to investigate, this reality, one might say, whose presence
> is supposed to be required by us....To this requirement correspond those radical
> points in the real that I call encounters, and which enable us to conceive reality
> as...*souffrance* ["in suspense," "in abeyance," "awaiting attention," "pending";
> and also "pain"]. Reality is in abeyance there, awaiting attention. (55, 56)

In Bausch's works, unexpected breakthroughs in re-presentation do not come as stage presence or fulfillment, but as moments of hesitation and emptiness. In another scene of *Mountain*, Dominique Mercy performs a series of repetitive movements of search and disappointment. Eventually, his instants of disappointment function as moments of suspension and non-representation.

Initially, Mercy's scene addresses the inefficacy of the search for an outside completion. To the sounds of a classical violin, he runs onstage with open arms, free flow, and indirect focus; his accelerated timing then slows down until he stops, bringing his arms down and arriving downstage right. Looking up past the audience, in a distant, fixed gaze, his eyes seem lost, or to be searching for something intangible and far from reach. He then runs to different spots of the stage, pausing each time to look past the audience. He is gradually joined by ten male dancers who spread out over the stage in a complex composition of running (acceleration), arrivals (deceleration), and hesitations (constant timing). The constant time evokes a feeling of emptiness in-between the unsatisfactory searches. Even with ten dancers spread all over, the stage does not seem filled, because the dancers evoke a sense that something is missing.

The dancers exit the stage and Mercy continues the sequence alone. The violin music stops, and he runs to downstage right, stops, and performs another variation of searching and hesitating. While gazing at the audience, he steps back tensely, grabs the bottom of his suit, hops once, and produces a forced smile, before becoming serious. His hesitation is reinforced by the stage's silence and emptiness. He seems unsure of what to do next, but certain that he should do something. He tries to fill performance time, but never really satisfies the audience's expectations for virtuosity or emotional expression. Therefore, he drops his smile and becomes serious in such an embarrassing situation.

He continues to hesitatingly repeat different acts as if to fill out performance time. He runs to different areas of the stage, lies down pretending to be dead, gestures as if trying to strangle someone, grabs a stick, tells a story about his hands, and does his fake smile and hopping routine.

Even Mercy's hesitations, which were initially a break in the chain of searches, became repetitive. Nonetheless, they are still not included in the signifying chain established by the previous repetitive movements. Instead, Mercy's hesitations contrast to the repetitive search and open it up. By staring at the audience and hesitating, Mercy interweaves the signifying chain with a kind of suspension. By repeating such suspension, he insists in its recognition as a break-through representation. In order to be acknowledged, non-representative time had to incorporate representative time's mechanism—repetition. Whatever Mercy does in fact conveys that he does not have anything to re-present. In a frightening moment, nothing seems to be really happening onstage. But it is in this "non-action" that the real takes place, transforming dance's disciplinary and productive time and space:

> The primary process [of the real]...must, once again, be apprehended in its experience of rupture, between perception and consciousness, in that non-

temporal locus, I said, which forces us to posit what Freud calls...the idea of
another locality, another space, another scene, *the between perception and
consciousness*. (Lacan 1978, 56)

Repetition initially conveyed dance as representation, separated from
the performer's "inward sensations" (chapter 3). Eventually, as in
Mercy's performance, repetition refutes dance's representative nature.
Mercy's hesitations neither present his inward sensations nor re-present
them. An empty space between the discourse of the unconscious (inward
sensations) and an apparent discourse (representation) gains its time for
expression. "It is within this vacuum, within this hollow, with what thus
becomes working materials, that the deep, secret discourse gains
expression" (Lacan 1988, 247).

Only through and within representation is dance able to momentarily
break its representative nature. We also see this happening in other
scenes of Bausch's pieces. For instance, the repetition of Benati's
increasing laughter in three different scenes of *Kontakthof* (chapter 3) at
first established re-presentation, and later linked different social
relationships by exposing them as dependency and desire. The third time
Benati laughed, it was followed by a long pause, no music, and not much
lighting or movement. This took over the stage space and time as a gap
on representation.

The same effect of Mercy's performance can also be seen in the
beginning of *Bandoneon* (1980), when Christian Trouillas hesitantly
walks around the stage, occasionally smiling at the audience and asking,
"Am I supposed to do something?", before abruptly leaving the stage. In
the second half of the same piece, a dancer comes onstage and provokes
the audience: "Do something!"   Such moments break through the
productive time of social disciplines, organized and imposed over the
body through repetition (chapter 4). In Bausch's dance theater, repetition
dismantles "Time measured and paid...without impurities or defects; a
time of good quality, throughout which the body is constantly applied to
its exercise" (Foucault 1995, 151). In such moments of hesitation, the
dancers question and disarrange the audience's expectations of a busy
and fulfilling performance. Heiner Müller argues that:

The public almost cannot stand pauses in the theater....Beckett; he gave exact
lengths to the pauses because he knew that directors and actors are afraid of
them. An actor is already scared stiff when he cannot move or say anything for

only ten seconds. It's against the arrangement. There is an arrangement, a rule: I pay and you work. The actor works, and I as a spectator pay. But I want him to sweat, this actor, for the money I'm paying him. If he doesn't do anything for a while, that means he's relaxing, the swine, on my money, and I won't have that. (1986, 23)

The fear of the underlying emptiness kept the dancers in a compulsive representation and the audience in an expectant mood. Facing the emptiness of non-representation promotes the recognition of the reciprocal dependency and absence. According to Sigmund Freud, "unconscious, mental processes are in themselves 'timeless'" (1959, 54). Mercy's timeless hesitations (constant timing) bring to consciousness a trauma previously experienced by both dancers and audience and repressed in the unconscious. Such suspensions of action reconstruct the first split between self and other, and the irretrievable fall into the Symbolic and repetition.

Repetition in Bausch's dance theater initially posits individuals, dance, and society within a signifying chain. Then, at unexpected moments, it takes them into their hollow essence. Repetition, as both means and subject, dismantles compulsive re-presentation at aesthetic and psychical levels. The response of dance critic Philippa Wehle to a multimedia scene of *Waltz* (*Waltzer*, 1982) describes the experience of such intolerable emptiness covered by representation in both life and theater:

[In the film clip] the newborn, still attached to its mother, lies on her stomach, and is softly touched, caressed and patted. The baby tries out its lungs, squirming and writhing in the pain and struggle of existence. We watch enthralled and horrified as the umbilical cord is cut and one more being is severed from safe union with another. This may be Bausch's celebration of life, but it is far from joyous. The party ends. A recording of Schubert's mournful *Impromptu* plays to an empty stage and the audience is left with pervasive feelings of sadness, emptiness and loss. (1984, 33)

6

"REDANCING" HISTORY:
RECONSTRUCTION AND TRANSFORMATION

To write is so many times to remind oneself of what never existed. How will I
succeed in knowing what I don't even know? This way: as if I had reminded
myself. With an effort of "memory," as if I had never been born. I was never
born, never lived: but I remember, and the remembrance is in live flesh.
Clarice Lispector (1992)

Repetition or Reconstruction of the Body Scheme?
Linear and Three-Dimensional Models of Time

The dancers of the Wuppertal Dance Theater often reconstruct onstage
scenes from their childhood. Such reconstruction unsettles preconceived
notions of presence and time, which fragment and control individual
bodies in both dance and society (Harvey 1989, 201–307). Throughout
this chapter, reconstruction implies a transformation in three levels: the
psychoanalytic (self/other), the aesthetic (dancer/audience), and the
temporal (past/future). The first two of these levels were explored in the
previous chapters, and the third will be covered in the following
discussion.

Since early Western philosophy, human existence in time has been
discussed as the relationship between permanence and change, between
repetition and renewal. For Heraclitus of Ephesus (c. 544–484 B.C.),
everything is in a constant state of change; things lack identity and only
exist as *Becoming*, without the permanence of *Being* (Guthrie 2000).
Time is a flux in which human beigs are included. But this permanent
impermanence follows an immutable cosmic law within (repetitive)
cycles of order. While Heraclitus defended Metaphysical Pluralism,
Parmenides (c. 540–470 B.C.) founded Metaphysical Monism, in which
the universe is comprehended as a single and permanent substance:
"What exists is akinêton—motionless" (Barnes 1982, 220).

Dealing with the paradox of the ultimate reality—being changing permanence—Plato (427–347 B.C.) stated the existence of a permanent essence of each mutable object (Hamilton and Cairns 1989). The object is and will always be an imperfect replica of its completed and fixed Ideal essence. In the Ideal sphere, change is abolished and time becomes an "eternal return":

> [For] the Greeks…[,t]he circular movement which assures the survival of the same things by repeating them, by bringing about their continuous return, is the perfect and most immediate expression (hence that which is closest to the divine) of the absolute immobility at the summit of the hierarchy. According to the famous Platonic definition, the time which is determined and measured by the revolution of the celestial spheres is the mobile image of immobile eternity which imitates by moving in a circle. Consequently both the entire cosmic process and the time of our world of generation and decay develop in a circle or according to an indefinite succession of cycles, in the course of which the same reality is made, unmade, and remade, in conformity with an immutable law and determinate alternations. The same sum of being is preserved; nothing is created and nothing lost; moreover, certain thinkers of dying antiquity— Pythagoreans, Stoics, Platonists—went so far as to maintain that within each of these cycles of time, of these *aiones*, these *aeva*, the same situations recur that have already occurred in the preceding cycles and will occur in subsequent cycles—and so ad infinitum. No event is unique, nothing is enacted but once…; every event has been enacted, and will be enacted perpetually; the same individuals have appeared, appear, and will appear at every turn of the circle. Cosmic time is repetition and *anakuklosis*, eternal return. (Corbin 1957, 40, 41)

Mircea Eliade defines such circular time as "mythical" (1988, 10). In it, the "primitive" or archaic human being ceaselessly repeats "the primordial act of the Creation of the World" (10). This model resists the internalization of history, instead positing an original, stable, and complete reality (Eliade 1974, 76–77).

Such a circular notion of time is inherent in ritualistic forms of dance. Differing from that religious context, circular time in contemporary staged dance-forms implies the dancers' belief that they repeat a moment of wholeness while technically moving onstage. Susan Leigh Forster refers to these dance forms as "natural" or "organic," associated with "a natural way of moving, a natural body, and a natural, organic choreographic process...[based on a cultivated] sanctimonious muteness...to champion the physical and the sensate" (1986, xiv–xv). It is implied that as the dancers experience fulfillment onstage, the audience is able to grasp the whole meaning of the dance. From this perspective, dance is the presence of bodies onstage. Nonetheless, such absolute presence or wholeness is based on its present absence—a unity experienced in a distant *past*.

For Aristotle (384–322 B.C.), the Ideal posited by Plato could be found in the empirical, sensed object as its *essence* (Kirwan 1971). In other words, lack of identity (Heraclitus's multiplicity and flux) and Being (Parmenides's uniqueness and permanence) were part of the same universe. In Aristotle's theory, all nature seeks to realize its essence—the Ideal goal—to fulfill its potentialities. Within this teleological framework, Aristotle divided time in a series of sequential "nows," in a linear and progressive construction (McKeon 1992, 122–145; Lütkehermölle 1994, 9). Such a notion of time can be represented by the spatial metaphor of a straight line. A sequence of "nows" builds a "progressive" time, going from a dismissed past toward an ideal future.

To Michel Foucault, linear, evolutionary time, "oriented toward a terminal, stable point" (1995, 160), characterizes the disciplinary method present in modern European schools, army, prisons, and factories:

> It is a question of extracting, from time, ever more available moments and, from each moment, ever more useful forces. This means that one must seek to intensify the use of the slightest moment, as if time, in its very fragmentation, were inexhaustible or as if, at least by an ever more detailed internal arrangement, one could tend towards an ideal point at which one maintained maximum speed and maximum efficiency. (154)

Such a straight linear time convention controls and determines the rhythm of individual bodies, creating a history of social coercion registered in the body through progressive repetitions. Through repetitive training, ballet and other social disciplines construct a straight linear notion of time in which the imperfect present body is constantly forced toward an ideal perfect future goal.

In dance, this notion of time validates the final product, which should resemble the choreographer's initial idea. Years of technical training and countless hours of rehearsals put in by the dancers are only implicitly part of the performance. In performance, dancers display incredible physical and technical abilities as if born with these god-given skills, while in fact they train rigorously to attain such high levels. The final presentation is prepared for the audience, although such dependency on the viewer is not explicitly included as a theme. This is true for most technical forms of dance, especially ballet.

While circular time posits an ideal past, this progressive model establishes an ideal future. However, both linear time frames do not recognize the inherent contradiction of the present as constant loss (absence). If the straight time-frame constructs a history of control over the body, the circular suppresses the recognition of this history, impeding its transformation. Both time frames resist social and aesthetic change. In staged contemporary dance, these time frames ignore the reciprocal dependency between dancers and audience, and the major contradiction of dance and all live performances—continuously disappearing as it is happening.

Repetition in Bausch's dance theater neither alludes to a linear progressive time nor takes the dancers back to a "primordial" state of unity. Repetition neither confirms nor denies the social constructions of time registered in the body. As discussed previously, her works consistently upset the progression of learning, expose the split between doers and watchers, and break through representation, bringing emptiness instead of wholeness. The repetition of a movement sequence causes more and more distortion, provoking multiple and unexpected interpretations and experiences. Included in history and language, dance is the absence, dissatisfaction, and constant reconstruction of itself and its participants.

In Bausch's pieces, the future does not repeat or distance itself from the past. Instead, the future transforms the past while repeating it, becoming a "retroactive working-through the past" (Žižek 1991, 189). The concept of "working through" was initially posited by Sigmund Freud, in relationship to his concepts of "repetition" and "recollection" (1963). Repetition takes place when patients reproduce the traumatic past only in their actions and do not deal with it in their memory or consciousness. Such behavior only brings more of itself, leaving the past traumas forgotten and repressed in the unconscious. "Recollection" is the reproduction of a past situation *in the memory* of the patient who is aware that such memory is distinct from his or her present life. Thus, such reproduction does not shake the patient's resistance to change and cure.

"Working-through" refers to a continuous process of living through resistance and repression as if within a "playground" (Freud 1963). It implies the recovering of lost memories, turning "repetition-reactions" into consciousness about one's own resistance. Jacques Lacan's theories complement those of Freud, by positing language—the Symbolic—as the means for working through the patient's resistance. Through language, the psychoanalytical dialogue between the patient (self) and the analyst (other) reproduces and transforms the patient's identity split. Both the patient and the analyst are questioned in a continuous process of repetition and transformation, "working-through language" (Lacan 1988, 157).

On an aesthetic level, Bausch's dance theater uses the same principle, questioning both dance and its participants, divided into doers (self) and watchers (other). The pieces are developed from the Symbolic reconstruction of the dancers' experiences in response to the choreographer's verbal stimuli (chapter 2). The creative process of Bausch's works begins with the translation of past experiences into language: "I didn't ask you to go there and cry. I asked you to try to think about what happens when you cry, the sounds....[In describing your laughter,] You must remain perfectly serious. I want to hear not how you laugh, but how you laughed, how you used to laugh in the past" (Wildenhahn 1982). The Wuppertal Dance Theater "rewrites history," as defined by Lacan:

> [T]he fact that the subject relives, comes to remember, in the intuitive sense of the word, the formative events of his existence, is not in itself so very important. What matters is what he reconstructs of it....The precise reliving— that the subject remembers something as truly belonging to him, as having truly been lived through, with which he communicates, and which he adopts—we have the most explicit indication in Freud's writings that that is not what is essential. What is essential is reconstruction....I would say—when all is said and done, it is less a matter of remembering than of rewriting history. (1988, 13, 14)

According to Lacan, since "a human gesture does belong with language" (255), here, "rewriting" can be equated to "redancing."

The reconstruction/transformation of the traumas of separation/split does not progress from the past to the future. The repressed traumas come "paradoxically from the future. [Traumatic] Symptoms are meaningless traces; their meaning is not discovered, excavated from the hidden depth of the past, but constructed retroactively" (Žižek 1991, 188–189). "[T]he patient has a future that you can move in the regressive sense" (Lacan 1988, 157). The traumas forgotten in the non-symbolic become included in the Symbolic order through such retroactive construction. They are then recognized by consciousness and become part of the subject's mutating retroactive history. This notion of Being that changes in a retroactive time was at first suggested by Martin Heidegger, using *Wiederholung* as "retrieval," instead of "repetition" (1962).

This retroactive process transgresses two-dimensional (linear or circular) notions of time, placing it in a three-dimensional spatial representation of an "internally inverted eight: a circular movement, a kind of snare" (Žižek 1991, 190; see figure 2, chapter 1). As a linear strip, instead of having its two edges (past and future) together (circular time) or far from each other (linear time), three-dimensional time has its edges twisted once before coming together. This creates a figure in which internal pathways become external and vice-versa. Such spatial construction represents a constant retroactive transformation of, and at the same time between, future and (inverted) past, as well as self (internal) and other (external). This twisted shape is part of Rudolf von Laban's theories of movement, described as the Lemniscate or Moebius Strip (1974, 98). This figure is drawn in space by a dancer performing simultaneous three-dimensional movements with two parts of the body. In Lacan's psychoanalysis, this "three-dimensional form of a torus" represents the fall into the Symbolic order and the subsequent construction of the body scheme (1977, 105). As the narcissistic ego's hollow essence, the Moebius Strip has an empty center.

Through reconstruction, the dancers of the Wuppertal Dance Theater "redance" their life experiences relating to the absence of the other and to fears of loneliness. They repeat the moments of split and lack with which they started to repeat and build their social and linguistic identities. Instead of returning to a fulfilling primordial past, the dancers advance toward a future (re)construction of their empty past. They integrate those moments of lack and search into symbolic language and consciousness, reconstructing and transforming the history of power registered in their (linguistic) body identities.

During the making of the piece *1980—A Piece by Pina Bausch* (*1980—Ein Stück von Pina Bausch*), Bausch asked the dancers pointed questions on their experiences of loneliness, search, and fear of darkness.

Subsequently, these themes found their way into the piece, in which dancers reconstruct these experiences in gestures and words.

In one of the scenes, Meryl Tankard runs tensely from down to upstage left, with her feet in half point. She wets her lips and looks backward at the audience while explaining in gestures and words: "When I go home at night, I get my lips really wet so I can scream, just in case somebody is behind me. And I run to the next apartment and ring all the bells to wake everybody up [demonstrating with the hands straight, tense, and quick], just in case somebody is behind me. And I run to the next apartment and ring all the bells to wake everybody up, just in case somebody is behind me. And I get my lips really wet so I can scream, just in case somebody is behind me." As she repeats this act for the third time, she runs toward downstage right. There, while demonstrating with a sleeping mat over the grass, she says: "When I go to bed at night, I look under my bed to see if anybody is under my bed. Then I get *in* my bed. Then I look *inside* my bed, just to see if anyone is *in* my bed."

Tankard's verbal phrases reconstruct more than a single event. They repeat her habits of repeating herself at specific repeated circumstances. The verbs are all in the present tense, under a condition of time ("when"). According to her description, she acted like that last night before going to bed, and will do it tonight, before going to bed. But the statements are made in the present tense, implying that they only exist as either past or future in the present. The words evoke a present reconstruction of simultaneously past and future repetitions. Paradoxically, such present is marked by absence. Tankard's repetitive actions are motivated by the search of the other, the absent persecutor, lover, and neighbors, all projected at the audience through the dancer's gaze.

In the scene, Tankard is clearly onstage enacting events placed outside the theater. But these everyday situations are as repetitive as any stage re-presentation. Stage representation is not opposed to daily life: Both are linked by their repetitive, linguistic, and "inauthentic" or non-unique constitution. The audience is constantly confounded, confronted with the absence of the other and of the re-presented events, while seeing live action taking place in the present. This scene, as with many other of Bausch's works, posits dance as inherently contradictory, by being simultaneously representative and experiential. Within the Lemniscate time-frame, such a scene reconstructs *another* moment of (artistic) creation, instead of returning to a "primordial" beginning. Within the Symbolic, this creative moment is not necessarily fulfilling, but provides experience and consciousness about its own paradoxical nature.

While Tankard is finishing her story, Anne Martin tells her own story to the audience as she enters downstage right. Her posture is slightly hunched and bent forward at the waist. Her eyes are quite attentive and dart toward different places in the theater. During most of her performance, her arms are tensely bent and held close to her upper body, with only slight movements toward the objects to which she refers: "When I was alone, I first checked that my bedroom was really locked; and I was so afraid that someone was hiding in my room! And that's why I looked under all the covers, under the table, under my bed, *especially* under my bed, to see if anybody was hiding there. And I was so afraid." She says the last sentence shrinking her torso, contracting her forehead, and smiling nervously. Throughout the story, her voice changes, indicating her excitement. Then, lying down on the grass, her body tight and straight, she holds her head off the ground and looks at the audience, continuing: "And then, I laid down, and covered myself really tight."

The public observes two distinct ways of expressing similar experiences. Both Tankard and Martin reconstruct a series of repetitive events triggered by absence and the desire for the other. However, Martin differs from Tankard by describing events in the past tense and by not illustratively acting out the scene. During most of her description, Martin stands downstage, and only slightly points at objects. Although not literal, her movements are intense, especially when she says she *was* afraid. Her present performance, with verbs in the past tense, overlaps the past and present, while the piece "progresses" to the future. Such overlapping recreates the audience's perception of time as a three-dimensional reconstruction of body memories.

As Martin finishes up her story, Mechthild Grossmann enters downstage right and speaks with her eyes wide open to the audience: "For more than thirty years I've been remarkably careful never to be alone in the dark ever. I couldn't stand it; I panic. Because of that, I always carry candles with me; especially when I travel. Abroad or overseas—never without my candles, ever; because of the electricity, you never know. And as a child, I was lying in my cradle, with all those bars, you know [gesturing toward imaginary bars]. And I got out, opened the kitchen door just a little bit, so that a little bit of light could come in.

And who came in? My nanny. And did she slap me! [She reacts to the "slap" with surprise, but then breaks into a slight smile—as if pleased by the experience]. And closed the door. I got out again, opened the door, she entered, and did she slap me! [She repeats the gestures] And so we went on and on, you know...I got out, opened the door, she entered, and did she slap me! [She repeats the sequence] So I'd rather be slapped than be alone in the dark; and never without my candles ever; because of the electricity, you never know. Me? Never. I, never. Never, ever."

Grossmann's scene describes the birth of a repetitive behavior. She repeats the moment in which she learned to be repetitive in both daily life and onstage. She initially exposed her adult mechanical routine, established by terms such as "never," "ever," and "always." Then she describes a childhood traumatic moment, which is consistently repeated as recurrent desire and need. However, Grossmann's performance establishes a three-dimensional time-frame in which childhood trauma and adult symptom are not cause and effect, but permeate each other within a repetitive signifying chain.

Grossmann's reconstruction, as well as those of the other dancers, may or may not cure their traumas. Though it transforms body memory into moments of "bodily consciousness"—Bausch's definition of dance (Servos and Weigelt 1984, 230; see chapter 1). Dance and the body are immersed in a constant Symbolic and historical flux. Differing from Heraclitus's constant state of change, Bausch's dance theater does not deny stability. Also differing from Plato and Aristotle, her works do not posit two categories of "appearance" and "essence." Within the Lemniscate, dichotomies of content-form, presence-absence, authenticity-repetition, health-disease, past-future become constant and reciprocal transformation.

Grossmann leaves the stage finishing up her story as Lutz Förster enters from the other side with his monologue: "I have never been afraid of the dark even as a child—never. When I was at home with my elder brother and there was a storm, big brother crawled into my bed. I took him into my arms and said, 'Uli, you don't need to be afraid, I'm with you!' Later we lived in Siegen, an isolated place. From the bus stop you had to walk ten minutes. No proper street, no houses anywhere, no street lights, past the small grove—it was not so bad. Only sometimes there were some strangers from the village watching. They did not like the people from outside. Even once they beat me for real. But my brother came to pick me up with a dog. And then they didn't appear. Then they simply kept their distance."

Differing from the other dancers, Förster's story displays courage, while his body gestures exhibit confidence. While Martin looked around, constrained and fearful, Förster alternates between a direct and indirect focus as if in control of his surroundings. During the creative process, each dancer reconstructs his/her peculiar personal experiences. This repertoire permanently becomes part of the piece. However, during subsequent performances of the piece over time, as the original dancers leave the company, new dancers take on these exact same characters. And the new dancers get to experience their own past through the original reconstruction. Ruth Amarante describes this experience as she substituted for Anne Marie Benati in the 1994 season of the piece *1980*: "It is her history, but I take it for myself. So, it is as if it were mine. My father died a long time ago, too, so it is very related with the loss of a close, dear person. It is not very far away [from mine]" (Amarante, appendix A; see chapter 2). Through symbolic reconstruction, personal stories become interpersonal experience.

In linear time, society invades the individual through a productive ideology. In circular time, individuals are caught in a constant repetition of the ahistorical, asocial, mythical moment of creation. The first opposed society to individuals, while the second covers or ignores such a dichotomy. In Bausch's works, within the Lemniscate shape of the Symbolic, individual and society do not erase or oppose each other: Both constantly (de)construct and (re)define each other.

In other moments of *1980*, the dancers also reconstruct their experiences of loneliness. In the beginning of the piece, Nazareth Panadero sits on a chair in a dim corner of the huge and empty stage. Wearing a long evening dress, she holds a cigarette lighter up to her chest, and looks at it; her face is serious, almost sad, while she sucks a candy. She flicks the lighter on and monotonously sings in a low voice: "Happy birthday to me." Then she blows out the flame, and says: "One." She repeats the same sequence, counting up to four.

Panadero ignites the lighter to commemorate the passing of the years. Nonetheless, these only echo as repeated marks of loneliness. The scene demystifies fire as a symbol of life and renewal. It shows this ritual and tradition of social commemoration as individual pain. It also upsets linear time by not providing a gradual progression toward a better future.

As in Jan Minarik taking balloons out of his trunks in *On a Mountain a Cry Was Heard* (*Auf dem Gebirge hat man ein Geschrei gehört*, 1984, chapter 3), Bausch confounds the audience's linear perception of time at the beginning of her pieces.

In *Dance Evening II* (*Tanzabend II*, 1991) Julie Shanahan stands on a table downstage wearing a bathing suit. She drinks water out of a bottle cap, dropping some of it on the table. She begins to talk to the audience while alternately kissing the wet table: "My father always kissed me like this before I went to bed. As quick as possible. I also wanted it to be as quick as possible. One, two, three. Little kiss, little kiss, little kiss. First he always passed his hands over the hair and then he smelled the hair and kissed—and smelled, and kissed. He always wet his lips completely and then kissed. One wanted to wipe it right away. Someone told me, that at that time the actors were not allowed to open their mouths while kissing. They always pressed their lips against each other's and made noises. I always rehearsed with my cousin, lips against each other—and making noise [she demonstrates]."

As in the previous examples, Shanahan's present reconstruction transforms her past: "It changes completely. People think of incest because of the other scene [with the cousin] that I put with it, but they are actually separated scenes....My father's kiss still remains a memory. But it changes in performance. I've kissed so many men in-between that experience and today, that somehow my father's kiss becomes different; it becomes other men's kisses. It all comes together on the stage scene. Originally, it is a happy memory, but in performance it becomes melancholic. I'm a lonely person talking about kisses I liked and kisses I didn't like, but they all become one because I did not find love" (Shanahan, appendix B).

In Shanahan's re-construction, previous experiences of touch are present as Symbolic traces of absence. This presents itself as break-throughs of productive disciplinary time, in moments of pause or slowness (chapter 5): "Something important about the whole scene—its very, very slow time. It can't be too slow because it disconnects, but it can't be faster either. Time goes on and on; it is very sensitive, very fragile" (Shanahan, appendix B). Similarly, Panadero's birthday scene, described earlier, evolves slowly, in the corner of a huge and empty stage. In many other scenes of *1980*, as in other pieces by Bausch, the stage is dimly lit similar to Grossmann's bedroom of her childhood memory. Such mournful environment is made up of a few dancers walking, dancing between empty chairs (*Café Müller*, 1978) or almost hiding in the background. This absent present provides space and time for the non-linear memories and associations of the dancers and the audience.

Café Müller is one of the few pieces performed by Bausch (figure 8). In the piece, the stage space is almost completely filled with coffee-shop tables and chairs. During the entire piece, Bausch has her eyes closed, and only perceptibly moves in certain scenes restricted to the right stage area. She is dressed in a white silk camisole, which together with her closed eyes creates an intimate atmosphere. She is almost imperceptible but nonetheless intriguing. She seems marginal to the events on central stage, as if she was a character dreaming them. The audience watches this personal dream become an aesthetic reality. According to Guy Delahaye:

> [Bausch's] parents had a restaurant. As a child, she liked to hide herself under the restaurant's tables, to be forgotten by her parents and to stay awake some hours more. Customers of the restaurant, who worked in the theater of the city, noticed her special way, her lightness. They took her to the infant ballet, and she studied there until fifteen years old. (1989, 7)

In *Café Müller*, Bausch seems to reconstruct those years of experience. However, as indicated by Slavoj Žižek (1991, 188, 189), the past is not hidden behind us, waiting to be excavated. Paradoxically, the past becomes what it always was only by its present symbolic reconstruction. So, instead of a restaurant full of people, as it was in her childhood, she reconstructs the space as it might be today after all these years.

Café Müller has six dancers who perform specific characters related to dance and to dance theater. Three of the characters—performed by Bausch, Malou Airaudo, and Dominique Mercy—represent "dancers," with abstract technical movements. These characters are mostly concerned with their inner impulses and not with the environment. The other three characters—performed by Nazareth Panadero, Jan Minarik, and Hans Pop (eventually substituted by Jean-Laurent Sasportes)— represent "dancers-actors," with functional or daily-life movements, always quite aware of their surroundings. While Bausch is bare feet and in only a camisole, Panadero is dressed in high heels, a big black coat,

Figure 8. Pina Bausch in *Café Müller*
© Photo by Alberto Roveri

in only a camisole, Panadero is dressed in high heels, a big black coat, and a curly red wig. Norbert Servos and Gert Weigelt explain: "The red-haired woman...is the questioning, searching woman of the dance theater...she embodies the more socially concrete, and thus the showier, more provocative theater of movement" (1984, 108).

At the last scene, Bausch and Panadero exchange roles. Panadero dresses Bausch in her red wig and heavy coat and leaves the stage. Now, alone at down and center stage, with her eyes still closed, Bausch stumbles into chairs, while the others dance upstage right almost unseen. From being a peripheral figure, Bausch becomes the center of attention. Dance and dance theater, initially represented by Bausch and Panadero respectively, become a single and lonely explorer in a dim, silent, and obstructive environment. However, underneath the thick coat of the searching dancer-actress, Bausch still wears her camisole. Her dance theater includes the intimate/personal (dance) and the social (theater) in a constant reciprocal transformation.

The dichotomy of a "pre-linguistic controlled body" versus a "linguistic controlling society" is dismantled. By including its controller's method (repetition) and subverting it, the body becomes responsible for its expression within the Symbolic. The means of domination (language) become a transforming/creative tool played through and by the body. Such a body is aware of its own history and is able to actively change it (Brandstetter and Völckers 2000). As stated by Servos and Weigelt, "[t]he body is no longer a means to an end. It has itself become the subject of the performance. Something new has begun in the history of dance: the body is telling its own history" (1984, 23).

By opposing itself as independent and complete, dance accepts its construction by the other—theater and words. Only then is dance able to reconstruct and transform such historical domination (Feher, Nadaff, and Tazi 1989). By accepting its otherness, dance becomes an emancipated agent of its own means—the body and movement.

Reconstructing the History of Dance

The Wuppertal Dance Theater reconstructs not only the history of the body, but also that of dance. Some of the company's pieces are critical interpretations of mythological or fairy tales, especially operas and

Romantic ballets. In these reconstructions, Bausch distorts the power relationships of the linear and verbal narratives, and substitutes them with the three-dimensional free association of body memory. The piece, *Bluebeard—While Listening to a Tape Recorder of Béla Bartók's Opera "Duke Bluebeard's Castle" (Blaubart—Beim Anhören einer Tonbandaufnahme von Béla Bartóks Oper "Herzog Blaubarts Burg,"* 1977; figure 9), was the first of Bausch's pieces to be created with the participation of the company members. In the creative process, Bausch asked the dancers about the story as they remembered it from fairy tales and particularly from Bartók's opera (1911), based on Charles Perrault's romantic ballet.

Bausch's choice of *Bluebeard* reveals her interest in the many levels of human relationships. The tale portrays a conflict in psychoanalytical, interpersonal, and theatrical dimensions. The image of Bluebeard's castle evokes his socially constructed narcissistic personality. This identity is constituted by the other in successive refusals/murders of itself. The latest wife goes in search of that past, which is, in fact, her future. Characters are fragmented and alienated within social gender roles. The opening lines of Béla Balázs's libretto for Bartók's opera (prologue) points to the split already described between self and other, content and form, woman and man, performers and audience:

> Hi, tune I hide,
> Where, where shall I hide it,
> It was, it was not: outside or inside?
> Old tune, hi, what does it mean,
> Men and women?
> ...
> You look, I look at you.
> Our eyes' curtain—the eyelashes—opens:
> Where is the stage: outside or inside,
> Men and women?
> ...
> The performance can begin.
> My eyes' curtain—the eyelashes—open.
> Clap when they close,
> Men and women.
>   (Bartók 1911, 177)

Figure 9. Beatrice Libonati and the
Wuppertal Dance Theater in *Bluebeard*
© 1996 Photo by Francesco Carbone

Differing from Balázs's interpretation of the tale, Perrault's text for the piece has a moralistic message that is radically transformed by Bausch. As stated by Katia C. Monteiro:

Perrault wrote *Bluebeard* as a warning message against feminine coquetry, stating the dangers of women's curiosity and disobedience....With Bausch, meaning is constantly scrambled and narrative evolution is replaced by extremely long repetitions. (1993, 195, 196)

Perrault's story includes two important repetitions: Bluebeard's successive disposals of his wives, and the message of perpetuating a socially submissive behavior. Bausch's reconstruction of such a repetitive past story incorporates repetition as its own means and subject. During the piece, Bartók's music is manually controlled on a tape player onstage by the protagonist (Jan Minarik, substituted by Hans Beenhakker, among others). Selected recorded fragments of the past become innumerable present moments. Toward the future, Bausch's reconstruction fragments and distorts the past.

The piece's last scene is particularly relevant in Bausch's interpretation:

Bluebeard lies over the woman's body while she is totally passive. He pushes her body against hers through the floor but she does not respond. She is already dead. He hugs her and claps as a way to wake her up, but she is deadly quiet. He then begins to clap desperately. His clapping suggests the obsessive acts of a child who acknowledges having done something wrong and therefore tries to undo it, playing as it was only a joke. At the same time, each time his claps stimulate the other dancers to move and freeze, which in itself is turned into a children's game. (Monteiro 1993, 231)

The poses taken by the group of dancers at each of Bluebeard's claps reconstruct earlier moments of the piece. They seem to be simultaneously rehearsing the sequences of scenes, or rewinding, this time, a "visual" tape of the performance itself. As performance time evolves, the piece approaches its end by retroactively showing posed pictures of earlier performed moments. Prompted by Bluebeard's claps, the dancers run and stop to pose more than fifty times. The running onstage is only a means of arriving at the desired goal—dance. And the dance consists of a few seconds of motionless poses.

Bluebeard's compulsion to repeat the past is exposed in his rewinding of the tape and in his clapping. His claps limit the time for the dancers' reconstruction of the scenes, creating new compositions of bodies in time and space. Instead of re-dancing the piece, they run and pause as in photographic bursts of memory, triggered by the stage applause in slow motion. Repetition becomes transformation in a non-linear time. The scene criticizes the counting to mark time done in technical dance. It subverts the exact repetition of timed movements marked by the choreographer or instructor. In such a manner, dance theater transgresses the disciplinary time of set choreography. Performance in present time is only possible as absence and flux, simultaneously evolving toward its end and "redancing" its past.

Bausch's works include and transform classically trained bodies (ballet) and the Socratic method of asking questions to draw the ultimate Truth (Irwin 1995). Within the Lemniscate, concepts contradict themselves, creating a state of constant redefinition and change. Repetition multiplies and erases itself, bringing transformation. Presence evokes absence, as Being becomes both to be *and* not to be (that is, indeed, the question). Preconceptions of Being and time, registered in our bodies, become contradictions and transformations within the unpredictable Symbolic search.

> Earlier I had wanted to be the others in order to know what was not me. I understood then that I had already been the others and this was easy. My biggest experience would be to be the other of the others: and the other of the others was myself. (Lispector 1992)

7

SPIRALING BODIES:
DIFFERENCE OVER DICHOTOMY

Why does one talk about dance alone? I cannot understand why the world is not included.
     Pina Bausch (quoted in Scheier, 1987)

It's that I'm perceiving a slanted reality. One seen through an oblique slice. Only now have I intuited the obliqueness of life. Before I saw only through straight and parallel slices. I didn't notice the artful, slanted trace. Now I divine that life is something else....Oblique life is very intimate....To live this life is more an indirect remembering of it than a direct living.
     Clarice Lispector (1989)

Repetition is a part of artistic representation and of social discipline. It establishes of a system of truths and social values. Bausch's dance theater radically alters such aesthetic and social means. In her pieces, the method unsettles final and "correct" interpretations or ideas. It is consistently used to subvert its own process of domination over the body. Bausch's use of repetition unsettles stable polarities of dominated-dominator, dancer-audience, movement-word, body-mind, woman-man, spontaneity-artificiality, everyday life-stage, individual-society, and meaning-form. These become dynamic modes of relationship, constantly questioning, and transforming aesthetic, psychic, and social roles.

Repetition dismantles dance as spontaneous expression. It then evokes experience by exploring dance's linguistic nature, performed by bodies just as needy and imperfect as those of the audience. Through repetition, the body explores its paradoxical existence, between natural and linguistic, experiential and automatic, personal and social. The body "retells" and "redances" its own history of domination, constantly repeating and transforming—"redefining"—dance.

Bausch's dance theater explores body memory between the sciences and the humanities. The three-dimensional shape of the Lemniscate can be expanded into the more complex format of a double DNA helix. Just as the DNA has four units that recombine unlimitedly, so does Laban

Movement Analysis with its four interrelated categories—Body, Effort, Shape, and Space (Hackney 1998). Laban's language of movement, as Bausch's dance theater, connects aesthetics and genetics as constant physical transformation. As the DNA, dance theater rewrites a three billion-year-old history:

> [T]he metaphor of a chemical text is more than a vision: DNA is a long, skinny assembly of atoms similar in function, if not form, to the letters of a book....The cells of our bodies do extract a multiplicity of meanings from the DNA text inside them....We must begin to see the texts of an individual and the texts common to members of a species as a form of literature, to approach them as one would approach a library of precious, deep, important books....Semiotics has given students of the DNA text a new eye for reading, allowing us to argue for the validity of a multiplicity of meanings, or even the absence of any meaning.... (Pollack 1994, 5, 6, 12)

This "chemical" text of atomic symbols is systematically repeated throughout a double helix, generating multiple or no meaning. It reproduces and recombines itself with precision, creating the new from the same. DNA and Bausch's dance theater follow the principle of *repetitiontransformation* (linked in the Lemniscate Shape). In genetics, as in the Wuppertal Dance Theater, one plus one equals many—genes, gestures, words, animals, people; carnations, grass, soil, water. Bausch changes globalization and cloning into difference and unpredictability.

Bausch demonstrates the creative use of unavoidable daily life compulsions. Her works provide a constant self-reflexive re-creation and re-definition of dance, individuals, and concepts. Bausch's aesthetic of *repetitiontransformation* does not deny or submit to elements outside dance. It includes and alters its otherness. In a reciprocal relationship, dance and movement alter and get altered by theater and words. Similarly, stage performance relates to the viewers' reactions, and technical traditions relate to everyday movement and popular culture. By including its other, dance becomes liberated from confining definitions and sources. Everything can turn into creative tools and materials. But this is not intended to transform daily compulsions into productive forces. On the contrary, repetition is used to dismantle functional power structures. It is a process of constant *artistic* re-creation in everyday life and in theater. In such aesthetically political perspective, anything can become the changing "dance" and "beauty."

As "bodily consciousness," Bausch's (definition of) dance recreates aesthetic, personal, and social history (Servos and Weigelt 1984, 230). The dancer is an intelligent, critical body. S/he is able to move and to speak, relating experience and language, practice and theory. Dance and life are not about positing or discovering Truth; instead, they are about questioning and playing with systems that predefine it. Above all, Bausch's works are about trusting the body—understanding and listening to its paradoxical and changing forms of knowledge.

The secret harmony of disharmony: I don't want what is already made but what is tortuously in the making. My unbalanced words are the luxury of my silence. I write in acrobatic, aerial pirouettes. I write because I passionately want to speak. Even though writing is only giving me the great measure of silence. (Lispector 1989)

APPENDIX A
INTERVIEW WITH DANCER RUTH AMARANTE
Translated from Portuguese
Wuppertal, June 1994

CF: Regarding the creative process, how much of it is Bausch's and how much of it is the dancers'?

RA: The old pieces, *Sacre*, *Blaubart*—well, in *Blaubart* she already began using the improvisation process—but *Iphigenia*, *Orpheus*, were all choreographed by her. I think that it started with *Blaubart*. She started asking the company-members questions, leaving it open as to how the person wanted to reply. You could answer in the form of movement, by talking, or by doing whatever you had in mind. It has been like that up to today. I think that earlier she interfered a bit more. But now she has left the people with much more freedom. She has a list that can go from 100 to 200 questions during a work. That is divided into two or three months, depending on the work, on the time she has to work. She asks one question, or even two questions in a period of two hours, four questions in a period of four hours. It isn't lots of questions, and she gives a good amount of time for the people to improvise.

CF: And can they answer several times?

RA: Yes, they can; several times or none—it is very flexible. Then she writes down almost everything—what she likes and what she doesn't like. And in the end she gives a list of the improvisations she liked most, to be repeated.

CF: To be repeated in performance?

RA: No, this is still during the creative process—in a later phase. Then we spend a long time just repeating improvisations. From these she further chooses some and says, in the end, in the very end, "try to put together this with this, this with that; try to do this with this other person." Then she starts putting things together like a game of dominoes, and at this point the work becomes hers. The final work is that of composition. Later, onstage, she starts to put together some scenes. Sometimes she places a person performing his/her scene, and lists a few things that could come after this scene. Then this person repeats the scene with something else, and then again with still something else, until

Pina sees what matches together well, and in this way she puts together the piece. This is a very simplified way of explaining it.

CF: Of course.

RA: In the meantime, Matthias [Burkert] chooses *several* songs and cassettes, and talks to her about it. During the improvisations, we don't have any music, except if someone specifically asks for it. It is during the final process of the piece that Pina starts experimenting with music. It can happen as it did in the last piece, *Ein Trauerspiel*. During the second act there were several different songs, and then on the day of the dress rehearsal she took them all out and put in Schubert's *Winterreise*. It was a shock for everybody. Nobody knows what may happen. During the time onstage, the first days, the first weeks, she still continues to change it; she does that up to today. Also, during the period of improvisation, there are days that she comes and gives us some movements. But they are quite small sequences or tiny movements, really small things. She gives three, four, five movements in one day. In the following day, she brings other movements. Something more or less like that. Sometimes there are also questions that she asks to be replied in form of movement. And she watches... Every improvisation is recorded on video. In the early days, it was not recorded. But nowadays we work with video when we do movements, so that we don't run into the danger of losing something that she liked. Then, in the end, she watches the video with you and says: "I liked this one, this one... Try to mix these things that I liked with the ones I brought you, and make up a dance." In the last three or four pieces, everybody has a little solo.

CF: Yes. I could see that in *Tanzabend II*. And about your creative process, when she asks you something...

RA: She asks everybody.

CF: Yes. How is *your* creative process? What comes first in response to the question—the emotion, the movement, or both simultaneously?

RA: It depends a lot on the question. It depends on what the question does to you. Sometimes, you have a total blank, you don't feel anything, you can't think of anything. In other times, you feel it right away. Suddenly, you find yourself going up front and saying something. Or it is a question for which you have to do a movement. It depends a lot on what is asked.

CF: Do you have some examples of the questions she asks?

RA: I have... to think! "Talking to a flower." "Mourning."

CF: So it is more a theme, not necessarily a question?

RA: It is a theme, it can be a question, it can be a tone..."Ah!" We already had this one. "Ah...my buttocks are so lonely." Things like this.

CF: And she does not move to instigate an answer; I mean, is it verbal?

RA: It is verbal. That has been my experience. I don't know if it was different in the beginning.

CF: Then you answer in the way you want.

RA: Yes.

CF: In these improvisation moments—would there be things from the past? Because several times onstage, I see children's stuff, or scenes.

RA: She asks other questions too, implying remembrance. I have to think about it now. Many questions are about how it was in our countries, culturally specific questions; how was our childhood... important people in our lives, about teachers, an important person in our lives or childhood...

CF: Then you create whatever you want on these themes?

RA: Whatever you want. Everything is very personal. There is lots of personal history in each improvisation. Sometimes it is not easy at all, especially for the new people who enter the company. I still haven't left the hard phase. Perhaps in the next piece it will become easier. But it is very hard. Sometimes there is a "click" and things start getting easy, but afterwards it returns to being difficult again. I mean—it is not the easiest thing in the world—no!

CF: So it looks like the questions instigate something else... Are there moments onstage that you do something from your past, something from your childhood or some memory?

RA: It is very hard because from all the improvisations—hundreds of them—she chooses one person's improvisation and asks this person to perform it in different ways. Sometimes she chooses specific improvisations from one person, but only fragments of them. She changes things a little; it is hard. I only did two pieces for a while with her. And the two pieces that I did were more dance/movement oriented. There is this scene in the last piece: I come running and dive into a bucket. For me, this has a lot of connection with the sea. It comes from the improvisation I did, in which I believe she asked "something that makes you very, very happy." For me, this was to dive into the sea.

CF: Sure.

RA: I mean, she didn't even imagine that this was what it meant. You don't need to explain what it means to her later. She just chooses what she likes.

CF: You went there, got the bucket, and created the improvisation from your own idea.

RA: Yes, it had to do with my history.

CF: In *1980*, the dancers run in circles around chairs, singing, playing children's game. What is it like for you as a Brazilian to play these children's games here [in Germany]? Is it somehow related to your childhood, or is it something totally German and totally off?

RA: No, I think it is not German at all. This game is only played in *1980*, in which these children's games are shown. Sometimes she asks questions about love games, for example. Especially for me this game of *1980* has a certain attraction because I lived for five years in the U.S.A., when I was a kid. So, there is a certain... This game was improvised by an American or an Australian woman.

CF: Somehow it provides you some experience?

RA: Yes. Even with the games being different, the feeling of the children's play is almost the same. You recognize yourself in it.

CF: And how is it when you perform it onstage? Is it something formal—a ballet?

RA: Of course. I joined in this piece long after it was completed. I mean, I'm doing someone else's role. So, in the beginning it is quite formal. You have to be in the right tempo, you have to take care not to get into people's way, you have to get the right chair in the right time, you have to do the movements—you have to do a bunch of things at the same time. So, in the beginning you get more the form of it. After some time, you start relaxing and then getting the feeling; the thing starts having a life of its own. When you have a lot of experience in the company, and do lots of this—getting someone else's role and having little time in which to do this—you pick it up more quickly; you start to manipulate feeling much better. It comes faster.

CF: The scene in *1980* in which you stand on the chair and tell the story of how your father used to dress you in your childhood...

RA: It is from Anne Marie Benati.

CF: I saw the original scene done by her, and also your performance. I found it amazing... very convincing. Looks like it is your own scene. Would this be an example?

RA: In the beginning it was hard, but now I am starting to find this little girl. I need a little time.

CF: Are you relating to her scene through your history, or are you getting into Benati's little girl?

RA: Both things. It is her history, but I take it for myself. So, it is as if it were mine. My father died a long time ago, too, so it is very related with the loss of a close, dear person. It is not very far away. I incorporate the role of another person like this, but this is not an *absolute* general rule. Each one works in a different way.

CF: And what about the fact that Bausch selected you to stay still while all the others perform individual farewells to you, also in *1980*?

RA: It is from Anne Marie. I took her role.

CF: In relation to repetitive movements: The dancer naturally creates it that way, or is it Bausch that asks him or her to do it over and over again?

RA: Uh... It depends.

CF: Or is it both things?

RA: In general, when the repetition is so obviously noticed by the public, then it is Pina's repetition. When we compose the solo, we repeat these little things a lot but mixed in-between others; you can't quite notice it. But when we repeat blocks of dance, repeating it again and again, it is more her theatrical conception. She likes repetition a lot. I believe she likes to mark the moment.

CF: When you substituted Beatrice Libonati for eight nights in Paris, how did it feel doing that repetitive scene of walking toward the wall, on all fours?

RA: It is a very hard role for me. Going on all fours to the wall, beating my head against the wall I don't know how many times, going, going, again and again... It was not easy for me to enter this role. It was the first time that I had to do a very bitter person, and I am a bit... I think... sweeter. Now I am starting to become bitter, I am learning. It was hard to engage in this bitterness. At the same time, I was having a personal crisis, and for eight performances, beating your head I don't know how many times against a wall per presentation... It is not only pain; it is this sensation of going toward the wall to beat your head, or wanting to go through the wall, and the wall being there, and repeating, repeating, repeating...

CF: Maybe it is different to do somebody else's movement several times. It probably gives a weird sensation. And what happens with a movement that you have created and Pina asks you to repeat several times? Has it ever happened?

RA: In the new piece, I lean my body against the wall; this was the only thing I did in the improvisation—I am "glued" to the wall. In the new piece I have to do this in the second act for twenty minutes, all the time.

CF: Was it Pina who asked you to repeat it?

RA: Yes.

CF: And what happens to you?

RA: Uh... It is totally crazy. It starts fine; it is a good sensation. But then it ends up being quite depressing; even for those who are just watching from the outside—a person that is there all the time, beating herself against the wall, falling down, and standing up, beating again on the wall, falling down on the floor... these are the things that she likes. I can understand what she likes in it. Because, when we dancers repeat the movements, at least we don't stay the same person as when we started. You change as well. And she appreciates this change with the same type of movement. It's just that... it hurts a lot sometimes.

CF: It brings some emotions?

RA: Yes, it does.

CF: From repetition itself?

RA: It is very, very loaded...

CF: Do you think it might produce some emotion different from that movement, or would it bring an emotion that is inside that same movement?

RA: If you take a movement and multiply it for I don't know how many times, I mean... the movement has a certain... it is loaded with possibilities and when you repeat it so many times, these possibilities grow and accumulate on each other.

CF: Intensity?

RA: Yes, I think that repetition changes the movement. You do it once, and it can be something completely different from what you do after twenty times.

CF: In *The Rite of Spring*, it looks like the dancers repeat and repeat and at the end they are very exhausted, as a result of repetition.

RA: Oh! That's an incredible experience!

CF: Because you are the "chosen" one, the one that is going to die?

RA: There isn't so much repetition in *Rite*. There is one repetition of beating on the ground, of beating myself, several times. But the whole solo is a progression. In that moment it is more startling—"What is happening?"—a mortal fear of death. It is as if no more blood were left in your brain.

CF: And you enter this completely, at an emotional level?

RA: Her interpretation is strange. The sacrificed could even feel honored and have some calmness. But in Pina's version, she wanted to show this instinctive fear of death.

CF: How did she bring it to you? Did she tell you anything during rehearsal?

RA: Later, later. First you learn the movements. She doesn't need to say much because the music gives you an incredible quantity, and the movements speak by themselves. In other words, she leaves you there for some time, to discover things a little by yourself. And then, she talks along during rehearsals.

CF: She only talks when you already know the sequences by heart?

RA: Everything. [She talks] when you already know everything and are now entering the feeling; the movement part is already a little clear.

CF: So the movement is first, and the feeling comes from the movement?

RA: Of course, because half of the feeling comes from the movement—it indicates where you have to go.

APPENDIX B
INTERVIEW WITH DANCER JULIE SHANAHAN
. New York, November 1994

CF: The scene from *Tanzabend II* in which you tell the audience about your father's kiss—How was it created?

JS: Bausch asked me to put things together. I had done separate improvisations earlier: with the bathing suit, with the glass of water, with kisses with my father, and with kisses with someone else. She told me afterwards to put together the talking [of the father's kiss scene] with the kisses on the table [from the scene of kissing someone else]. She asked an improvisation, and I just did a composition, putting together the three improvisations. In the scene, I drink out of the cup, and then drop water on the table and kiss the table, while talking about kisses. It is a very important memory. It is the memory of my first kiss, and it is not with my mother. It is with my father.

CF: And what happens to your personal memory by making a theatrical scene out of it, and by performing it on stage?

JS: It changes completely. People think of incest because of the other scene [with the cousin] that I put with it, but they are actually separated scenes. It looks like melancholy. [In rehearsal,] I did not know if I was answering what Bausch had asked. I didn't do it for an audience. I did it as talking to myself, about myself. It is very personal. My father's kiss still remains a memory. But it changes in performance. I've kissed so many men in-between that experience and today, that somehow my father's kiss becomes different; it becomes other men's kisses. It all comes together on the stage scene. Originally, it is a happy memory, but in performance it becomes melancholic. I'm a lonely person talking about kisses I liked and kisses I didn't like, but they become one because I did not find love. Also, this scene is connected to the one soon after, in which I measure the different parts of my body, standing on the table. It is sad; searching for some kind of perfection... You end up lonely even though you are so perfect and beautiful.

CF: As more you perform this piece, what happens to you during this scene?

JS: The first time I performed it, I did not know how I would react. I became aggressive toward the audience. They probably didn't even understand it. Also because, at the same time, Geraldo [Si Loureiro] is drawing and crossing hearts on his body, looking at audience members. They might think what I do is somehow connected to his scene. Then, it was becoming more and more familiar to me each night. You can then go deeper in the feelings. One main thing about the company's creative process is that even though you are talking about memories, you are still an actress and it is in the piece. Other scenes may happen at the same time of my personal story, without having anything to do with my life; also other dancers can eventually do this scene about my father's kiss. Something important about the whole scene—its very, very slow time. It can't be too slow because it disconnects, but it can't be faster either. Time goes on and on; it is very sensitive, very fragile.

WORKS CITED

Artaud, Antonin. *The Theater and Its Double*. Trans. Mary Caroline Richards. New York: Grove Press,1958.

Banes, Sally. *Writing Dancing in the Age of Postmodernism*. Hanover, Conn.: Wesleyan University Press, 1994.

Barnes, Jonathan. *The Presocratic Philosophers. The Arguments of the Philosophers*. Ted Honderich, ed. New York: Routledge, 1982.

Bartenieff, Irmgard. "The Roots of Laban Theory: Aesthetics and Beyond." In *Four Adaptations of Effort Theory in Research and Teaching*. New York: Dance Notation Bureau, 1970, 1–28.

———. *Body Movement: Coping with the Environment*. Langhorne, Penn.: Gordon & Breach Science Publishers, 1980.

Bartók, Béla. *Bluebeard's Castle: Opera in One Act* [*A Kékszakállú herceg vára*], text Béla Balázs. 1911. Music Score. Reprint. Christopher Hassall, trans. New York: Boosey & Hawkes, 1952.

Bausch, Pina. *Arien*. 1985a. 150 min. Next Wave Festival, Brooklyn Academy of Music Opera House, New York. Videocassette.

———. *Café Müller*. 1985b. 60 min. Wuppertal Opera House. Suhrkamp Verlag. Videocassette.

———. *Carnations*. 1986/1987. Wuppertal Opera House. Program. Trans. Rainer L. Brueckheimer.

———. *Don't Be Afraid*. 1985c. 83 min. Next Wave Festival, Brooklyn Academy of Music Opera House, New York. Videocassette.

———. *Kontakthof*. 1985d. 173 min. Next Wave Festival, Brooklyn Academy of Music Opera House, New York. Videocassette.

———. *1980—A Piece by Pina Bausch*. 1984. 156 min. Sadler's Wells Theatre, London. Channel Four/ZDF. Videocassette.

———. *On the Mountain a Cry Was Heard*. 1985e. 137 min. Next Wave Festival Opera House, Brooklyn Academy of Music Opera House, New York. Videocassette.

————. *The Plaint of the Empress*. 1989. 99 min. Inter Nationes. Videocassete.

————. *The Rite of Spring*. 1985f. 35 min. Next Wave Festival, Brooklyn Academy of Music Opera House, New York. Videocassette.

————. *The Seven Deadly Sins*. 1985g. 45 min. Next Wave Festival, Brooklyn Academy of Music Opera House, New York. Videocassette.

Baxmann, Inge. "Dance Theatre: Rebellion of the Body, Theatre of Images, and an Inquiry into the Senses of the Senses." *Ballet International* 13(1): 54–61 (January 1990).

Benjamin, Walter. "The Work of Art in the Age of Mechanical Reproduction." In *Illuminations*, ed. Hannah Arendt, 217–251. New York: Schocken, 1976.

Bentivoglio, Leonetta. "Exits & Entrances. Pina Bausch's *Palermo, Palermo*." *Artforum* (April 1990): 19–20.

————. *O Teatro de Pina Bausch*. Lisbon: Acarte/Fundação Calouse Gulbenkian, 1994.

Birdwhistell, Ray L. *Introduction to Kinesics*. Louisville, Ken.: University of Louisville Press, 1952.

————. *Kinesics and Context*. Philadelphia: University of Pennsylvania Press, 1970.

Bowie, Malcolm. *Lacan*. Cambridge, Mass.: Harvard University Press, 1991.

Brandstetter, Gabriele, and Hortensia Völckers. *ReMembering the Body*. Ostfilden-Ruit, Germany: Hatje Cantz Publishers, 2000.

Brecht, Bertolt. *Brecht on Theatre: The Development of an Aesthetic*, trans. John Willett. New York: Hill and Wang, 1979.

Caputo, John D. *Radical Hermeneutics: Repetition, Deconstruction, and the Hermeneutic Project*. Bloomington: Indiana University Press, 1987.

Connor, Steven. *Samuel Beckett: Repetition, Theory, and Text*. New York: B. Blackwell, 1988.

Corbin, Henry. *Man and Time*. New York: Pantheon Books, 1957.

Darwin, Charles. *The Expression of the Emotions in Man and Animals*. 1872. Reprint. Francis Darwin, ed. Chicago: University of Chicago Press, 1965.

Delahaye, Guy. *Pina Bausch*, trans. Rainer L. Brueckheimer. Cologne: Bärenreiter, 1989.

Deleuze, Gilles. *Difference and Repetition.* New York: Columbia University Press, 1994.

Derrida, Jacques. *Writing and Difference.* Chicago: The University of Chicago Press, 1978.

Durán, Cristina. "Teatro-Dança de Pina Bausch faz 20 Anos." *O Estado de São Paulo* IX (2.768), 7 September 1994, *Caderno 2.*

Dürrenmatt, Friedrich. *Plays and Essays.* New York: Continuum Publishing Company, 1982.

Edwards, James. *The Authority of Language: Heidegger, Wittgenstein, and the Thread of Nihilism.* Tampa: University of South Florida, 1990.

Eliade, Mircea. *The Myth of the Eternal Return, or Cosmos and History.* Trans. Willard R. Trask. Princeton: Princeton University Press, 1974.

————. "The Eternal Return." *Parabola* (spring 1988): 4–15.

Erler, Detlef. *Pina Bausch.* Zurich: Edition Stemmle, 1994.

Feher, Michel, Ramona Nadaff, and Nadia Tazi, eds. *Fragments for a History of the Human Body.* New York: Urzone, 1989, 3 vols.

Foster, Susan L. *Reading Dancing: Bodies and Subjects in Contemporary American Dance.* Berkeley: University of California Press, 1986.

Foucault, Michael. *Discipline and Punish: The Birth of the Prison.* 2nd ed. New York: Vintage Books, 1995.

————. *The Birth of the Clinic: An Archeology of Medical Perception.* 2nd ed. New York: Vintage Books, 1994.

Freud, Sigmund. *Beyond the Pleasure Principle.* New York: Bantam Books, 1928, repr. 1972.

————. "Further Recommendations in the Technique of Psychoanalysis: Recollection, Repetition, and Working-Through (1914)." In *Therapy and Technique,* ed. Philip Rieff, 157–166. New York: Collier Books, 1963.

————. "The Uncanny (1919)." In *On Creativity and the Unconscious,* 122–161. New York: Harper & Row, 1958.

Goldberg, Marianne. "Artifice and Authenticity: Gender Scenarios in Pina Bausch's Dance Theatre." *Women & Performance—A Journal of Feminist Theory* 2(8): 104–117 (1989).

Goldberg, RoseLee. *Performance Art: From Futurism to the Present.* 2nd ed. London: Thames & Hudson, 2001.

———. *Performance: Live Art since the 60s.* London: Thames & Hudson, 1998.

Grosz, Elizabeth. *Jacques Lacan: A Feminist Introduction.* New York: Routledge, 1990.

Guthrie, W.K.C. *A History of Greek Philosophy.* Vol I. *The Early Presocratics and Pythagoreans.* Cambridge, UK: Cambridge University Press, 2000.

Hackney, Peggy. *Making Connections: Total Body Integration through Bartenieff Fundamentals.* Amsterdam: Gordon & Breach Science Publishers, 1998.

Hamilton, Edith, and Huntington Cairns, eds. *Plato: The Collected Dialogues, Including the Letters.* Princeton: Princeton University Press, 1989.

Harvey, David. *The Condition of Postmodernity: An Enquiry into the Origins of Cultural Change.* Cambridge, UK: Basil Blackwell, 1989.

Haskell, Barbara. *BLAM! The Explosion of Pop, Minimalism, and Performance, 1958–1964.* New York: Whitney Museum of Art, 1984.

Heidegger, Martin. *Being and Time.* New York: Harper & Row, 1962.

Hillman, David, and Carla Mazzio. *The Body in Parts: Fantasies of Corporeality in Early Modern Europe.* New York: Routledge, 1997.

Hoghe, Raimund. "The Theatre of Pina Bausch." *The Drama Review* 24(1): 63–74 (March 1980).

Hoghe, Raimund, and Ulli Weiss. *Bandoneon—Em que o Tango Pode Ser Bom para Tudo?* São Paulo: Attar, 1989.

Howe, Dianne S. "The Notion of Mysticism in the Philosophy and Choreography of Mary Wigman 1914–1931." *Dance Research Journal* 19(1): 19-24 (summer 1987).

———. *Individuality and Expression: The Aesthetics of the New German Dance, 1908–1936.* New York: Peter Lang, 1996.

Hutchinson-Guest, Ann. *Your Move: A New Approach to the Study of Movement and Dance.* Langhorne, Penn.: Gordon & Breach Science Publishers, 1983.

Irwin, Terence. *Plato and Socrates' Meno: Plato's Ethics*. New York: Oxford University Press, 1995.

Jeschke, Claudia, and Gabi Vettermann. "Germany—Between Institutions and Aesthetics: Choreographing Germanness?" In *Europe Dancing—Perspectives on Theatre Dance and Cultural Identity*, eds. Andrée Grau and Stephanie Jordan, 55–78. New York: Routledge, 2000.

Kamper, Dietmar. "Incorporation and Mimesis: Primordial Patterns of Imagination." In *Binationale: German Art of the Late Eighties, American Art of the Late Eighties*, eds. Jürgen Harten and David A. Ross, 46–50. Cologne: DuMont Buchverlag, 1988.

Kawin, Bruce F. *Telling It Again and Again: Repetition in Literature and Film*. Niwot, Colo.: University of Colorado Press, 1989.

Kerkhoven, Marianne van. "The Weight of Time." *Ballett International* 14(1): 62–69 (January 1991).

———. "Dance, Theatre, and Their Hazy Boundaries." *Ballett International* 1: 30–35 (January 1993).

Kew, Carole. "From Weimar Movement Choir to Nazi Community Dance: The Rise and Fall of Rudolf Laban's *Festkultur*." *Dance Research Journal* 18(2): 73–96 (winter 1999).

Kierkegaard, Søren. *Fear and Trembling; Repetition*. 1843. Princeton: Princeton University Press, 1983.

Kirwan, Christopher, trans. *Aristotle's "Metaphysics."* Oxford: Clarendon Press, 1971.

Kristeva, Julia. "Gesture: Practice or Communication?" In *The Body Reader: Social Aspects of the Human Body*, ed. Ted Polhemus, 264–284. New York: Pantheon Books, 1978.

———. *The Kristeva Reader*. New York: Columbia University Press, 1986.

Laban, Rudolf von. *Die Welt Des Tänzers*. 1920. Reprint, Stuttgart: W. Seifert, 1926.

———. *Laban's Principles of Dance and Movement Notation*, ed. Roderyk Lange. Boston: Plays, 1975.

———. *Rudolf Laban Speaks about Movement and Dance: Lectures and Articles*, eds. Lisa Ullmann and Surrey Addlestone. London: Laban Art of Movement Centre, 1971.

————. *The Language of Movement: A Guidebook to Choreutics*. Boston: Plays, 1974.

————. *The Mastery of Movement*, ed. Lisa Ullmann. Plymouth, Mass.: Northcote House, 1988.

Lacan, Jacques. *Écrits: A Selection*. New York: W.W. Norton & Company, 1977.

————. *The Four Fundamental Concepts of Psycho-Analysis*. New York: W. W. Norton & Company, 1978.

————. *The Seminar of Jacques Lacan* Book I. *Freud's Papers on Technique, 1953-1954*. New York: W.W. Norton & Company, 1988.

Langer, Susanne K. *Feeling and Form*. New York: Charles Scribner's Sons, 1953.

Lispector, Clarice. *Para Não Esquecer*, trans. Sonia Roncador. São Paulo: Editora Ática, 1979.

————. *The Stream of Life* [*Água Viva*], trans. Elizabeth Lowe and Earl Fitz. Minneapolis: University of Minnesota Press, 1989.

Lütkehermölle, Matthias. "Blurring the Line: Derrida on Heidegger on Time, Presence, and Metaphysics." M.A. Thesis, New York University, 1994.

Maletic, Vera. *Body—Space—Expression. The Development of Rudolf Laban's Movement and Dance Concepts*. Berlin: Mouton de Gruyter, 1987.

Manning, Susan. *Ecstasy and the Demon: Feminism and Nationalism in the Dances of Mary Wigman*. Berkeley: University of California Press, 1993.

Markard, A., and H. Markard. *Jooss*. Cologne: Ballett-Bühnen Verlag, 1985.

McEvilley, Thomas. "Pina Bausch." *Artforum* (October 1984): 85–86.

McKeon, Richard, ed. *Introduction to Aristotle*. New York: The Modern Library, 1992.

Monteiro, Katia C. "The Fairy Tale Revised: A Survey of the Evolution of the Tales, from Classical Literary Interpretations to Innovative Dance-Theater Productions." Ph.D. Diss., New York University, 1993.

Moore, Carol-Lynne, and Kaoru Yamamoto. *Beyond Words: Movement Observation and Analysis*. New York: Gordon & Breach, 1988.

Müller, Heiner. "A Talk Beneath Language." *Ballett International* 9(12): 22–28 (December 1986).

Osborne, Claire. "The Innovations and Influence of Rudolf Laban on the Development of Dance in Higher Education During the Weimar Period (1917–1933)." In *Working Papers*, vol.#2, 83–102. London: Laban Art of Movement Centre, 1989.

Partsch-Bergsohn, Isa. "Dance Theatre from Rudolph Laban to Pina Bausch." *Dance Theatre Journal* 6(2): 37–39 (July 1988).

————. *Modern Dance in Germany and the United States: Crosscurrents and Influences. Choreography and Dance Studies Series*, vol.#5. London: Harwood Academic Publishers, 1994.

Phelan, Peggy. "The Ontology of Performance: Representation without Reproduction." In *Unmarked: The Politics of Performance*, 146–166. New York: Routledge, 1993.

Pollack, Robert. *Signs of Life: Language and Meanings of DNA*. Boston: Houghton Mifflin Company, 1994).

Preston-Dunlop, Valerie. "Laban and the Nazis." *Dance Theatre Journal* 6(2): 4–7 (fall 1988).

Prevots, Naima. "Zurich Dada and Dance: Formative Ferment." *Dance Research Journal* (spring/summer, 1985): 3–8.

Ragland-Sullivan, Ellie. *Jacques Lacan and the Philosophy of Psychoanalysis*. Chicago: University of Illinois Press, 1986.

Raven, Arlene. "Everyone into the Water—*Arien*." *High Performance* 32: 75 (1985).

Roth, Moira. "Pina Bausch: The Seven Deadly Sins." *High Performance* 33: 78–79 (1986).

Samuels, Robert. *Between Philosophy and Psychoanalysis: Lacan's Reconstruction of Freud*. New York: Routledge, 1993.

Saussure, Ferdinand de. *Course in General Linguistics*. Paris: Payot, 1916. Reprint. Charles Bally and Albert Sechehaye, eds; Roy Harris, trans. La Salle, Ill.: Open Court, 1986.

Scarry, Elaine. *The Body in Pain: The Making and Unmaking of the World*. New York: Oxford University Press, 1985.

Scheier, Helmut. "What Has Dance Theatre to Do with *Ausdruckstanz*?" *Ballett International* 10(1): 12–17 (January 1987).

Schlicher, Susanne. *TanzTheater Traditionen und Freiheiten*. Hamburg: Rowohlt Taschenbuch Verlag, 1987.

————. "The West German Dance Theater: Past from the Twenties to the Present." In *Choreography and Dance* vol.#3, part 2, ed. Suzanne K. Walther. London: Harwood Academic Books, 1993.

Schmidt, Jochen. *Tanzen gegen die Angst: Pina Bausch*. Munich: Econ & List Taschenbuchverlag, 1998.

Schmidt, Jochen *et al. Tanztheater Today: Thirty Years of German Dance History*. Seelze/Hannover: Kallmeyersche, 2000.

Sebeok, A., and Jean Umiker-Sebeok, eds. *Nonverbal Communication, Interaction, and Gesture*. New York: Mouton Publishers, 1981.

Servos, Norbert. "Pathos and Propaganda? On the Mass Choreography of Fascism: Some Conclusions for Dance." *Ballett International* 13(1): 62–67 (January 1990).

————. *Pina Bausch—Wuppertaler Tanztheater oder Die Kunst, einen Goldfish zu dressieren*. Seelze, Germany: Kallmeyersche, 1996.

Servos, Norbert, and Gert Weigelt. *Pina Bausch Wuppertal Dance Theater or The Art of Training a Goldfish: Excursions into Dance*. Cologne: Ballett-Bühnen-Verlag, 1984.

Tate, J. "Imitation in Plato's Republic." *The Classical Quarterly* #22: 16–23 (1928).

Vaccarino, Elisa, ed. *Pina Bausch: Teatro dell' Esperienza, Danza della Vita*. Genova: Edizioni Costa & Nolan, 1993.

Varnedoe, Kirk, and Adam Gopnik, ed. *Modern Art and Popular Culture. Readings in High & Low*. New York: The Museum of Modern Art/Harry N. Abrams, 1990.

Vogel, Walter. *Pina*. Munich: Quadriga, 2000.

Walther, Suzanne K. "The Form of Content: The Dance Drama of Kurt Jooss." Ph.D. Diss., New York University, 1990.

————. *The Dance Theatre of Kurt Jooss. Choreography and Dance*, vol.#3. London: Harwood Academic Publishers, 1993.

————. *The Dance of Death: Kurt Jooss and the Weimar Years*. London: Harwood Academic Books, 1994.

Warr, Tracey, ed. *The Artist's Body*. London: Phaidon, 2000.

Wehle, Philippa. "Pina Bausch's Tanztheater: A Place of Difficult Encounter." *Women & Performance—A Journal of Feminist Theory* 1(2): 25–36 (winter 1984).

Wigman, Mary. *The Language of Dance*. Middletown, Conn.: Wesleyan University Press, 1966.

Wildenhahn, Klaus, dir. *What Do Pina Bausch and Her Dancers Do in Wuppertal?* 1982. 80 min. Inter Nationes. Videocassette.

Wright, Elizabeth. *Postmodern Brecht: A Re-Presentation*. New York: Routledge, 1989.

Žižek, Slavoj. "The Truth Arises from Misrecognition." In *Lacan and the Subject of Language*, eds. E. Ragland-Sullivan and M. Bracher, 188–212. New York: Routledge, 1991.

INDEX

Ciane Fernandes in *CorPoesis Prematurus* (São Paulo, 2000);
Costume by Márcia Ganem; Photo by Euler Paixão

Ciane Fernandes is a tenured professor in the Performing Arts Graduate
Program at the Federal University of Bahia, Brazil, and an associate researcher
at the Laban/Bartenieff Institute of Movement Studies (LIMS), New York. She
received a Ph.D. in art and humanities for performing artists from New York
University (1995) and a certificate of movement analysis from LIMS (1994).
She is the author of *The Moving Body: The Laban/Bartenieff System in
Performing Arts Education and Research* (2002). She has danced and choreo-
graphed in the United States, Italy, and Brazil, and has published articles in
Brazil and Germany. She is Director of the AFFECTUS Dance Theater Group
at the Federal University of Bahia, which in 2000 received the Brazilian
ANDES-SN National Prize for Art at Universities. She has been awarded with
several scholarships and prizes, including a 2003 Virtuoso Grant from the
Brazilian Ministry of Culture to further develop her latest project: a compar-
ative study between contemporary dance theater and the classical Indian
dance style of Bharatanatyam at the Rajyashree Ramesh Academy for
Performing Arts, Berlin.

NEW STUDIES IN AESTHETICS

Robert Ginsberg, General Editor

Victor Yelverton Haines & Jo Ellen Jacobs, *Associate Editors*

This series publishes explorative thinking in the philosophy of art as well as in the philosophy of life. Applied aesthetics and theoretical development of non-traditional topics are considered, along with traditional studies in aesthetic theory or the problems specific arts. Well-written volumes may take the form of monographs, treatises, collected essays, proceedings, reference works, and translations. Use of illustrations is encouraged. In addition to works in English, texts in German, French, Spanish, Italian, and other languages may be published.

For additional information about this series or for the submission of manuscripts, please contact:

Peter Lang Publishing, Inc.
Acquisitions Department
516 N. Charles St., 2nd Floor
Baltimore, MD 21201

To order other books in this series, please contact our Customer Service Department:

(800) 770-LANG (within the U.S.)
(212) 647-7706 (outside the U.S.)
(212) 647-7707 FAX

BROWSE ONLINE BY SERIES AT WWW.PETERLANG.COM